Notes On Interior Design

William Kaufmann, Inc.

95 First Street

Los Altos, California 94022

ISBN 0-86576-021-7

This book is a product of Information Design Associates: Larry Belliston, Kurt Hanks, Information Planners; Jay Parry, Editor; David Bartholomew, Production Art and Typography; Sue Parker, Richard Moore, Research Assistants; Randy Stroman, Rodney Showtrow, Illustrators.

10 9 8 7 6 5 4 3 2 1

Experimental Edition
Readers who wish additional information or who have suggestions for changes, and/or other improvements are invited to write to the publishers who will appreciate any such material and will share it with the authors.

INTRODUCTION

■ These notes on interior design represent more than twelve years of professional work in the field. During that time we have taught hundreds of college students, written three texts for the design field, and spent several years in actually making the principles of interior design work. Through that practical experience we participated in the interior design of dozens of residential and commercial projects.

■ That experience has shown us how absolutely crucial a good understanding of the basic principles of design are to professional success. Skills are more important than facts, but *principles* must act as a foundation for both. No matter what you plan to do with your basic understanding of interior design—whether to become a professional in the field, to work in a related field of graphic design or architecture or even fine art, or to simply use your knowledge to enhance your day-to-day living—a good grasp of the basic principles is essential. It's for that reason that we emphasize those principles in the notes.

■ You can tell at a glance that this is a very visual book. There are two big reasons why we've attacked this subject in that way. The first is that people learn more if they're *shown* as well as *told.* Evidence is very convincing that a picture really can be worth a thousand words, especially if that picture is carefully chosen and wisely presented. The second reason is that interior design is a very visual field. It's a subject that would be impossible to learn without strong visual support. To try to do otherwise would be a mistake.

■ Our purpose, as you have probably already discerned, is not to provide a deep treatise on the principles of interior design. Rather it's to give an introduction, a beginning point. The serious student will want to take what he learns here, build upon it and add his own notes.

■ Use this book as a beginning to expand your own increasing knowledge of the profession of interior design.

CONTENTS

DESIGN

de·sign (di-zin′), *v.t.* [OFr. *designer;* L. *designare,* to mark out, define; *de-,* out, from + *signare,* to mark < *signum,* a mark, sign]. **1.** to plan; make preliminary sketches of; sketch a pattern or outline for. **2.** to form (plans, etc.) in the mind; contrive. **3.** to plan to do; purpose; intend. **4.** to intend or set apart for some purpose. *v.i.* **1.** to make designs. **2.** to make original plans, sketches, patterns, etc.: as, she *designs* for a coat manufacturer. *n.* [Fr. *dessein;* It. *disegno < disignare;* L. *designare*], **1.** a plan; scheme; project. **2.** purpose; intention; aim. **3.** a thing planned for or outcome aimed at. **4.** a working out by plan: as, do we find a *design* in history? **5.** *pl.* a secret or sinister scheme (often with *on* or *upon*): as, he has *designs* on her property. **6.** a plan or sketch to work from; pattern: as, a *design* for a house. **7.** the art of making designs or patterns. **8.** the arrangement of parts, details, form, color, etc., especially so as to produce a complete and artistic unit; artistic invention: as, the *design* of a rug. **9.** a finished artistic work. —*SYN.* see **intend, plan.**

THE PURPOSES OF DESIGN

Design is a purposeful activity. It is not an end in itself but is a means for accomplishment. It is a tool for change towards meaningful objectives. Among the purposes of design are:

■ To organize elements into unified wholes.

■ To bridge the gap between things and people.

■ To improve our human accommodation with our physical surroundings.

■ To decrease the cost of the creation and maintenance of an item.

■ To increase the safety of interactions between people and their environments.

■ To increase the efficient use of things.

■ To save time and materials and provide optimal utilization.

■ To act as a means of enhancing communication.

KEY POINTS ON DESIGN

■ Organization is the essence of any design. But doing nothing is also a form of design. It is hazardous to design by neglect and default. We cannot afford the human and material costs that almost always result from solutions that ignore conscientious design.

■ Design sometimes suffers from a dilemma about its identity. It is not solely either an art or a science but is a combination of both. Design isn't like physics or biology or writing or painting, but it involves these areas and more. Design tends toward a generalized approach, collecting specifics from diverse areas as needed. Design is a combination of art, science, technology, and intuition.

■ Design does contain sound, proven principles and criteria for judging its success. These criteria center around the relationship between human needs and human environmental possiblities. The measure of the success of a particular design is how well it meets the needs of the people experiencing it. Good design is matching the best decision to the given situation. It is finding the optimum solution for the parameters that have been set.

YOU ARE A DESIGNER

■ Whether you've been trained or not, you are sometimes a designer. If you haven't been exposed to the principles of design before, chances are that you're pretty poor at the job! But you are a designer nonetheless. You pick out your clothes, considering shape, color, and price. All those are elements of design. You select the paint for your living room wall, deciding the color, the texture, the sheen. You select the furniture and fixtures that go in the room. You decorate the walls with paintings or ornaments. In all this you are acting as a designer.

DESIGN—A MATTER OF SCALE

Design permeates our existence. The principles apply on every level, though the scale may change. The illustration below suggests some of the major areas of design.

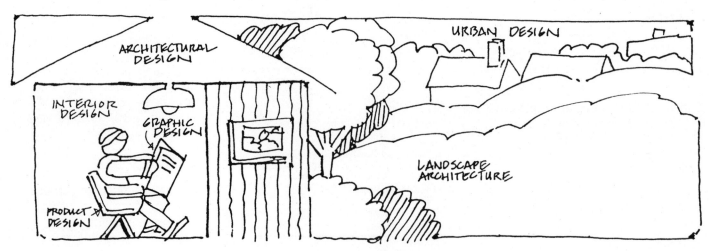

INTERIOR DESIGN

THE PURPOSES OF INTERIOR DESIGN

- Interior design is a goal-centered activity, It is not an end itself but a means to achieve particular effects.

- Interior design is concerned with the immediate human environment and how it affects the user. The designer must also consider how the environment is affected by that user.

- Interior design renders our living, working, and playing areas more attractive and useful. Interior designers attempt to create environments that will at the same time support human activities and be aesthetically pleasing.

- Interior design is not a fine art—though it is akin to one. The fine artist deals with aesthetics. The interior designer deals with that and more. The designer is also much concerned with function. He combines art with technology to create environments or objects that are usable as well as enjoyable.

- Interior design is something that is *used* by living human beings, with all their needs, wants, habits, frailties, and inconsistencies. The success of a designer's work can be judged accurately only within the human context.

There are three main areas of creation in interior design. They are interrelated, but each demands a unique knowledge and ability. Many interior design firms do a combination of all three.

KEY POINTS ON INTERIOR DESIGNERS

- Interior designers plan and supervise the design and arrangement of building interiors and furnishings.

- Interior designers seek to create an atmosphere congruent with the user's lifestyle.

- The interior designer makes the best use of the space available.

- The interior designer needs a thorough understanding of the building process. This enables him to draw plans that can be economically constructed, to supervise the actual construction or fulfillment of those plans, and to establish the critical details that make the difference between success and failure.

- The interior designer must be familiar with all the techniques and tools of spatial organization. His task is not so much to create something new as it is to collect elements and arrange them within a particular environmental context.

- Interior designers are design generalists. Their purpose is the creation of the optimal interior environment, using many areas of specialization. Knowing the possible elements of interior design and understanding all the possible arrangements becomes critical.

- Interior designers must learn to *see* the end result of their work, in their minds, before it becomes reality. They must learn to envision and solve all possible problems before the actual work of creating begins.

- Interior designers need to have "people skills," as well as knowledge of principles and materials. Remember, the designer does not work in a vacuum, but rather creates and molds environments to meet the needs of the users. He must be able to work and communicate well with clients, suppliers, contractors, associates, and other involved professionals.

RESIDENTIAL	COMMERCIAL	SPECIAL
• The living environment, the home residence, where we spend most of our time, (about (1/3 of it asleep) • Critical need to understand the owner's needs, family lifestyle, and relationships to their environment	• The working environment, the office, business enterprise, contract work (we spend about 1/3 of our time working) • Critical need in the relationship of the interior environment to worker needs and perceptions, and productivity	• The specialized environment serves unique design functions: i.e., airplane and automobile interiors, restaurants, theaters, hospitals, exhibits, and other special designs • Critical need for understanding of the uniqueness of the product or service and its connection to the user or buyers

HISTORY

	79*		1000		1500		1600		1700

ANCIENT	PALEO-CHRISTIAN BYZANTINE	GOTHIC	RENAISSANCE	BAROQUE
EGYPTIAN GRECIAN ROMAN WESTERN ASIA				

FRENCH PERIODS

FRENCH PROVINCIAL

LOUIS XIV

ENGLISH PERIODS

ELIZABETHAN   JACOBEAN   WILLIAM & MARY

COLONIAL

*SPACING BEFORE 1500 A.D. IS NOT TO SCALE.

■ Interior design has its roots in the architecture, fine arts, and crafts of the past. It is a natural human desire to create a pleasing environment. But interior design is a relatively new field, a field that began with the concern for home "decoration." In the past few decades, interior design has emerged as a profession, reaching the status of architecture.

GOTHIC (1000–1300)

The dominant interior shapes and forms were strongly linked with contemporary architecture. Particularly influential were the Gothic arch and the religious motifs of Gothic churches and cathedrals. In general, furniture was of oak, and the stiff, vertical tendency of the design made the interiors feel solemn and majestic. Each country, however, adapted the Gothic approach to its own needs. Hence, in Italy the decor was rounded and religious; in France, it was refined and graceful; in England, it was solid and rugged. In this style, dovetail and miter joints were frequently used. Works of art were essentially religious in theme.

RENAISSANCE (1480–1630)

This period originated in Italy, where designers returned to classic Roman and Greek lines. The design tendency shifted from vertical to horizontal. Decoration and ornamentation became free and obvious. Walnut was the favored wood. The art of veneering was perfected. This period marked the rebirth of art throughout Europe, indicating the end of the Dark Ages. The period includes Elizabethan as well as early Jacobean styles.

AMERICAN PERIODS

EARLY AMERICAN DINING CHAIR

EARLY AMERICAN OR COLONIAL (1607–1776)

Furniture reflected the styles of each builder's native land, though styles were simplified for economic and technical reasons. Plain, sturdy pieces were the norm, built out of oak, maple, pine, or other locally available woods. Upholstery was rare. Utility was generally the first consideration, with pieces serving dual purposes. Architecture was rough and practical.

4

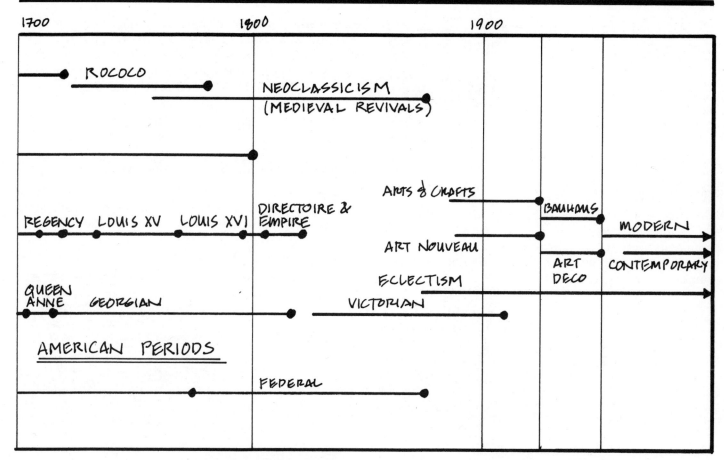

1700   1800   1900

ROCOCO

NEOCLASSICISM
(MEDIEVAL REVIVALS)

ARTS & CRAFTS   BAUHAUS

REGENCY   LOUIS XV   LOUIS XVI   DIRECTOIRE & EMPIRE   MODERN

ART NOUVEAU

ART DECO   CONTEMPORARY

ECLECTISM

QUEEN ANNE   GEORGIAN   VICTORIAN

AMERICAN PERIODS

FEDERAL

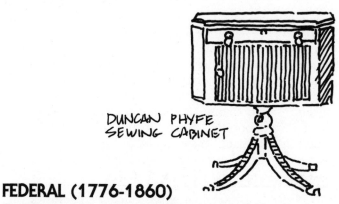

DUNCAN PHYFE
SEWING CABINET

FEDERAL (1776-1860)

Buildings were constructed in a revival of classical style. Greek columns (Doric, Ionic, Corinthian) were popular, both in outside architecture and interior design. Interior columns were used to divide rooms and support mantlepieces. Classical decorations were common inside and out. Much of the distinctive furniture was in the Duncan Phyfe style, which was characterized by fine proportions, a combination of curved and straight lines, and a lyre, eagle, or plume motif. Mahogany was the predominant wood, though maple, oak, walnut, and cherry were also used.

ENGLISH PERIODS

ELIZABETHAN (1533-1603)

This period is named after Queen Elizabeth I of England. Furniture was of heavy oak; designs were rigid; legs and supports were huge and swollen.

JACOBEAN (1603-1688)

Furniture was primarily of oak, still following the rigid designs of the Elizabethan period, though it was designed more for comfort. Ornamentation was heavy. Some Renaissance influence is evident. The design can particularly be seen in heavy chests, tables, and chairs. Needlework and tapestry were used in the upholstery. This period is named for the Jacobites, who were an English political group in power during the period.

WILLIAM AND MARY (1689-1702)

The Dutch influence was strong during this period, which was named after the Dutch monarchs William and Mary who reigned over England for the years indicated. Furniture was mainly of walnut and oak; it is characterized by soft, curved lines. The style is seen in cabinets, occasional tables, and small chairs. The trumpet leg and cupped foot were introduced.

QUEEN ANNE "ROUNDABOUT" CORNER CHAIR

QUEEN ANNE (1702-1714)

Curvilinear lines became the norm, with the cabriole leg and pad foot appearing on the furniture. Comfort and simplicity were the watchwords. Woods used included walnut, pine, ash, and oak. Some Oriental influences can be seen.

CHIPPENDALE "CHINESE MOTIF"

GEORGIAN (1714-1830)

This period is named for four kings of England, Georges I, II, III, and IV, who served in succession. Mahogany, satinwood, and rosewood were the primary woods used. Dominating the period were four furniture designers: Thomas Chippendale, who combined Gothic, Chinese, and Rococo details; Robert Adam, who was noteworthy for his classical ornaments and painted wood; George Hepplewhite, noted for his rich upholstery and dainty chair legs; and Thomas Sheraton, whose graceful designs were characterized by uncommon sturdiness.

REGENCY (1810-1820)

This period is characterized by floral designs and Chinese motifs. Chairs, tables, sofas, and beds were all influenced by the period; legs were usually straight but sometimes fluted. Mahogany and rosewood were the primary woods used. They were combined with black and gilt paints to produce the total effects. This period was strongly influenced by the classical period that was occurring in France at the same time.

VICTORIAN (1837-1901)

This period, named after Queen Victoria of England, is cluttered with machine-made furniture of awkward design. Styles were commonly mixed with unpleasing effect. Some stalwart designers struggled, primarily in vain, to revive the fine styles of the Georgian period. Their work was characterized by full curved lines and elaborate decor. Some Victorian chairs are upholstered and have an oval back with a carved wooden frame.

FRENCH PERIODS

FRENCH PROVINCIAL (1500-1800)

During this period, cabinetmakers adapted the styles of the Paris court to the needs and pocketbooks of French people in the provinces. The style was solid and graceful; they had little if any ornamentation or inlay.

LOUIS XIII WRITING TABLE

LOUIS XIV (1643-1715)

Rich, lavish, large-scale furniture, made primarily out of oak, walnut, and chestnut, marked this period. The furniture was heavily ornamented; decorations often borrowed from the Baroque. Much of the furniture was painted in vivid colors. Damask upholstery and satin brocades were popular. Straight lines dominated. The theme of this period was *excessiveness*.

FRENCH REGENCY (1715-1723)

While Philip II, Duke of Orleans, ruled as regent for the child-king Louis XV, the ornate styles of the previous period were modified. More restraint was shown in the design of the furniture; colors were softened; decorations were less obtrusive.

LOUIS XV (1735-1774)

During this period the restraint that was introduced during the French Regency period was dropped, with designs returning to the lavishness of the Louis XIV period. Costly inlays and rich Chinese lacquers became the norm. Cabriole legs and scroll feet were part of the design. Mirrors were introduced as part of the dressing tables. The principal woods used were mahogany, oak, rosewood, and tulipwood. The Rococo influence first began in this period.

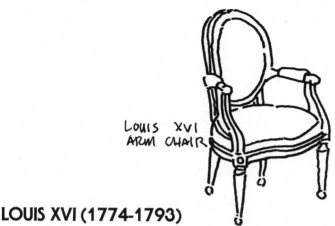

Louis XVI Arm Chair

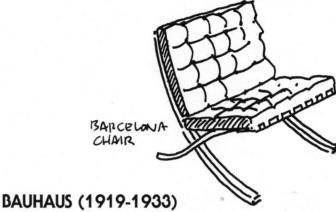

Barcelona Chair

LOUIS XVI (1774-1793)

This period experienced a return to the classic feel of Greek and Roman art. Legs of the furniture were straight, being tapered and reeded. Wood was marked with classic details, inlays, and painted decorations. Rose carvings and trims were popular, following the preferences of Queen Marie Antoinette. The Rococo influence continued.

DIRECTOIRE (1795-1799)

The Napoleonic era began here, and the French immediately overthrew the traditional. Cottons and chintzes replaced satin upholstery. Frivolous decor was replaced by revolutionary symbols, such as liberty caps, staves, pikes, and joined hands. Mahogany, rosewood, and oak were used in a simple and pure style.

FRENCH EMPIRE (1799-1814)

During this period Napoleon continued his reign, and decorations included such symbols of victory as could be borrowed from Egyptian and Roman cultures. Napoleon's emblem, the bee, was much in evidence. Classic Greek and Roman influences were still present in the style, but in severe styles lacking soft curves. Furniture had tapered pillar legs or round legs with ball feet.

OTHER PERIODS

ART NOUVEAU (1890-1914)

This period was marked by a revolt against nineteenth-century historicism. Symbols were used on the furniture to blend naturalistic and aesthetic elements. Pieces of furniture were often painted; designs and forms became sharper. Tiffany lamps date from this period.

ARTS AND CRAFTS (1885-1915)

This movement advocated a deliberate disregard for technology and progress. Its hallmark was sturdy, honest construction and craftsmanship. It was believed that form must follow function. Very little ornamentation was used.

BAUHAUS (1919-1933)

A response to the Arts and Crafts movement, designers in the time of Bauhaus contended that art could be unified with technology, that aesthetically pleasing objects could be made by mechanical means. The Bauhaus movement began in Germany, but quickly spread.

Eames Armchair & Ottoman

MODERN (1942-present)

The Modern period grew out of the Bauhaus movement. With the idea that technology was a friend rather than an enemy, designers found new options in such materials as plastics, metals, and glass. Woods tend to be natural-colored. Planes and surfaces are kept simple; lines are low. The key criterion in the Modern period is *functionalism.*

Parson's Table

CONTEMPORARY (1950-present)

Contemporary is a modification of the Modern style. In Contemporary, designers have combined the function and materials of the Modern approach with the elegance and flavor of a more historical style. Classical and traditional forms are borrowed freely, including historical motifs and carvings. A feeling of Old World artistry is sought.

CLIENTS

Clients are of critical importance to interior design. You wouldn't go into the field if you didn't enjoy it. But how will you be able to afford such a job? The client will pay for you to practice your skill. Without clients there would be no such profession. The more effective a designer is in meeting a client's needs the more satisfying his interior design business will be.

■ All to often interior designers have trouble with their clients. Or, to be more fair, we can say that clients have trouble with their interior designers. Remember that in the end the client, who holds the purse strings, is the man or woman who is in charge of the job and who will own the design. If you'll take care to have good relations with clients and to meet their needs, you'll find that everyone is better served. And, in the end, you will be much more successful in your profession.

STRIVING FOR HARMONY

■ If you hope to be successful in your interior design, you'll need to be a master of *harmony*. You'll need to do a balancing act between several forces: your own desires and the client's; the ideal design and the design he can afford; the aesthetic and the functional. As you become more and more experienced you'll grow more and more proficient in that balancing act. But always you should remember the vital importance of the *client*.

THE ELEMENTS OF THE DESIGN SITUATION

DESIGNER — ENVIRONMENT — CLIENT

■ Let us reiterate something here: an interior designer's job is not to create great art, nor is it to utilize the latest thoughts in design. Rather, his job is to use his skill to the best of his ability to create the very best design possible while still meeting the needs of the client. The designer who meets his client's needs will be in business for a long time. His design skills are important, yes, even crucial. But they'll do him absolutely no good if he doesn't use them to effectively serve the client.

WORKING WITH A CLIENT

■ Getting the client to work with your firm is a process that involves seven steps.

CONTACT
Establish your initial contact with the client. This can usually be done by mail or by telephone. Tell the client about previous work you've done and mention any references he may want to check.

INTERVIEW
Next you set up an interview, so you can personally convince the client that you are the one for his job.

RAPPORT
Once you are sitting across the desk from the client, take care to establish a rapport with him. A good relationship will go along way to your being able to land a job.

CREDIBILITY
But rapport won't do it all. You also need to show the client that you have the ability to do the job. Establish credibility here. Show him your portfolio and resume, so there won't be any doubt as to your design experience and ability.

DEFINE
Once he's indicated a desire to work with you, take the trouble to define the scope of your services. Rather than losing you the job, this will help cement it for you. Talk very specifically with the client about what you will do, and what he is expected to do. Find out how much money the client is willing to commit to the job. This kind of discussion will solve a lot of problems later.

COMMIT
Now's the time to make a commitment. Sign on the dotted line, indicating that you're willing to work within the restraints of the job, including finances and time deadlines. It's also often a good idea to have the client sign a simple contract, indicating that he does indeed desire your services and is willing to pay the specified amount.

REVIEW
Your contact with the client isn't over once you've started the job, of course. The seventh step is crucial: to have periodic reviews with him. You need to give him feedback about how the job is going; and he needs to give you feedback about how he feels. The final point of feedback is when the job is completed. There the client gives his final approval for the job and makes his final payment for your services.

CLIENT PROFILE

■ With every new client you have, it would be helpful if you drew up a client profile, asking yourself several questions. Every human being you'll ever meet is made up of many different components; and a complete understanding of your client will come only when you understand many components of his being.

■ The more you're able to understand your client, the more you'll be able to meet his needs. And the more you're able to meet his needs the higher regard he'll have for your abilities.

PROFILE QUESTIONS

■ Consider these 6 critical areas: physical, intellectual, expectational, emotional, motivational, and economical, one at a time. Then combine them into a unified whole.

■ What kinds of people are clients? A more accurate way to put the question would be: What kinds of entities are clients? Oftentimes the designer finds himself dealing with organizations as much as with individuals. And who are these organizations and individuals? Here's the beginnings of a list:

- Home owners
- Government agencies
- Department stores
- Furniture stores
- Antique dealers
- Architects
- Hotel/restaurant chains
- Home furnishing magazines
- Builders and developers
- Manufacturers of furnishings & textiles
- Select, specialized businesses, such as airplane and car manufacturers, for interiors

■ Here are the questions you should consider, along with some questions you should ask about your client:

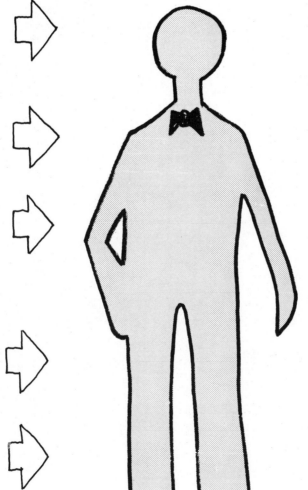

PHYSICAL: What are their physical needs? What are their body requirements?

EMOTIONAL: What are their emotional needs? If they have any hang-ups that would relate to your design, what are they?

INTELLECTUAL: How do they view themselves intellectually? How do they view the process and product of design? How easily do they absorb and accept new principles and new concepts?

MOTIVATIONAL: What are their reasons for seeking an interior design? How deep-seated are those reasons?

EXPECTATIONAL: What kind of results are they expecting? How firm are they in those expectations? How crucial is it that those expectations be met?

ECONOMICAL: What kinds of funds do they have to work with? How limiting will their economic circumstances be on the design you create? What does their economic condition tell you about the end result you should expect? Do their expectations match the amount of money they have or are willing to spend?

SOCIAL: How do they relate with others? Neighbors? What size groups? What social space configuration is needed?

CULTURAL: What are the unique cultural aspects of space? Do certain cultural elements need to be added? How does this project fit into the broader cultural framework?

DESIGN PROCESS

■ The process of design moves by stages from conception to completion. There are several design approaches, but all involve the following steps:

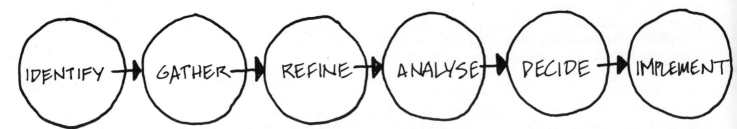

1 **IDENTIFY** the problem. Here you see what needs and criteria the design must meet. This step generally involves stating the requirements, defining the limitations, and listing applicable data.

2 **GATHER** preliminary ideas. This is the most creative segment of the process. Once you understand the problems, you're able to begin generating ideas. You can get your mental process going by reviewing solutions others have come up with, doing research, brainstorming, or listing questions and then putting down the answers. Some small, quick sketches at this point will help.

3 **REFINE** the ideas you've produced. Here you examine each idea carefully and either accept or reject each one. In doing so you'll be making decisions that will affect the rest of the project. Make your judgments according to the needs and criteria you've already established. At the same time, consider economy, resourcefulness, and aesthetics. Enlarge and refine your interior sketches.

4 **ANALYSE** the ideas you have remaining to determine which works best. At this point you'll create working models of the solution.

5 **DECIDE** on one solution. You've gone through all the previous steps, gradually working from nothing to a working model or two. Now make your decision: Is the design successful? Or do you need to return to step 1?

6 **IMPLEMENT** your decision. Make the interior designs become reality. Here you get final approval from the client (including both cost and plans), order the furnishings, supervise the work of subcontractors, and so forth.

■ There are other things to keep in mind when working through the design process:

CHANGES The design changes with each design problem. You will find that, even though you utilize the six steps of the design process, your process solution will require continual changes. Look for changes and develop your own modified process for each design.

FEEDBACK Each design you complete gives you new insights that can be applied to future problems. It's a repeating cycle of design, feedback, design, feedback. Experience is a good teacher, and it's a wise student who can learn from his own experience. An even wiser person will be able to get feedback and vital information from the experiences of others and not waste time duplicating research or mistakes.

PROJECTION A designer must always look ahead in the design process. He should temper the design process steps, by seeing himself moving toward the approaching end result. Interior designers' key motivating skill is the ability to see the finished project in their minds at the very beginning of their creative effort, which provides the needed continuity between the process and the final product.

■ The Design Process can express itself in more than one arrangement. At the top of the page is a linear process. Still others are possible:

CYCLIC PROCESS Process moves in a cycle with no clear beginning or ending point.

BRANCHING PROCESS Certain stages trigger process growth in more than one direction.

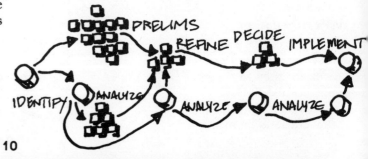

SOURCES

■ A big part of the interior designer's job is to arrange multiple elements from many sources into one cohesive whole. More than any of the other design and architecture professions, interior design relies on information and samples from manufacturers and distributers. Usually the interior environment is full of detail and demands a large amount of time-accounting and refinement. Effectively managing these materials and sources is critical to the design results that are often demanded.

BUYER AND LIBRARIAN

■ With the number of product categories and varieties of color, finish and quality, the creation of a source library is mandatory. This product information storage and retrieval system, full of sample and catalog data, needs continual control and updating.

■ The writing of specifications for such varied items as picture frames and rugs can get quite involved. This often requires a different role than many beginning interior designers anticipate. New technical language and detail skills are required.

■ Financial skills also enter into the design development process. The designer often has the role of a shopper or buyer, purchasing from a large number of manufacturers and suppliers. The responsibility of quality control becomes critical as well.

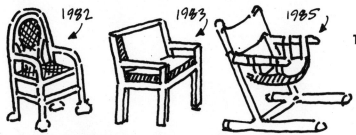

■ These materials, information and samples are in a continual state of flux. New furniture styles, fabrics and patterns are always being created. The choices and changes possible often make a hard job seem impossible. But the more you know about what is available and how it can be used, the better choices you can make and the more functional, beautiful and original your designs can be.

■ Most materials, furniture accessories and surfaces are selected from swatch books and catalogs from manufacturers or suppliers. Swatch books are usually interchangeably bound or linked together with other relevant information (pictures, descriptions and specifications) from each source.

FINDING SOURCES

■ How do you get to these sources? Try the following methods:

OTHER INTERIOR DESIGNERS Talk to other successful and qualified designers in your geographic and interest area. Professionals in design are often very helpful. Their experience enables them to filter out for you the irrelevant and unsuccessful materials and sources.

SOURCE CATALOGS These are collections of a variety of suppliers, distributors, and manufacturers under accessible headings. The best are *The Sweet's Design File* and a *Contract Interiors* catalog.

THOMAS REGISTER The Register is a gold mine. It is a huge collection of the nation's manufacturers listed by what they make. Sources may be found there that cannot be found elsewhere. Most libraries have a set.

MAILING LISTS Put your name on mailing lists for interior designers. A lot of the mail you get will be junk, but occasionally in comes just what you're looking for. Usually a letter requesting information will put you on the list. Such lists are shared among similar sources.

LABEL AND TAG An interior designer is always looking in stores, showrooms, restaurants, etc. When something strikes you, check the back label and write the name and address down. Then the source information is yours.

TRADE SHOWS AND SHOWROOMS Many manufacturers and suppliers have locations where you can see and feel the materials and furniture. Permission to attend these events and visit these sources is critical. First-hand experience is a lot better than any photo in a product looseleaf.

HUMAN SCALE

■ An interior designer arranges physical elements for humans, and thus everything he does should be adapted to "human" scale. Too often designers neglect to take this scaling into consideration; they are more concerned with the aesthetic than the functional. It's possible, however, to create a design that allows for both aesthetics and function. The designer must keep in mind that both are criteria for acceptable design.

WHAT DOES HUMAN SCALE MEAN?

■ It means that everything you design must fit well with the human mind and body. In other words, fit the environment to its user. If you fail in that, you fail in everything, since a design that doesn't fit is unusable—and an unusable interior design, no matter how attractive, is, to speak frankly, good for nothing.

THE PROPER FIT

■ You've seen people whose clothes didn't fit too well. Maybe the knees in the pants were too baggy; maybe the shoulders were too full. If the collar size was too small the person wasn't able to button it to wear a tie. If the collar was too large he could button it—but it hung out around his neck like an unsightly moat. The solution? Tailor the suit of clothes—and the design—to the person using it.

■ The same kind of problem exists when a designer doesn't account for human scale. The design won't *fit*, and the result will be unsightly and unusable. The user will feel uncomfortable in that particular interior.
Make sure you get the user's environmental clothes to fit him.

ENVIRONMENTAL INFLUENCE

■ There are several factors to consider in designing for human scale. The first is environmental influence. For instance, a human being has very definite reactions to such factors as noise, light, temperature, humidity, and ventilation. There is a range in each where the person can function comfortably. This is called the range of acceptance. Once you move outside the range of acceptance, you've created a design that is, for practical purposes at least, unusable.

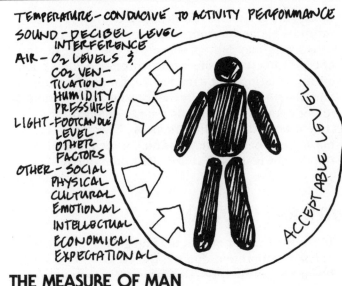

THE MEASURE OF MAN

■ Human adults do not grow ten feet tall, nor are they two feet tall. Typically they will range from five feet to seven feet in height. Their weight range also falls within a definable range—say, from 100 to 300 pounds. Certainly there are exceptions at both ends of the height/weight range, but the general range gives you parameters you can use in your design. If you don't consider those parameters, your design won't have the necessary physical fit, and it will, in the end, be unusable.

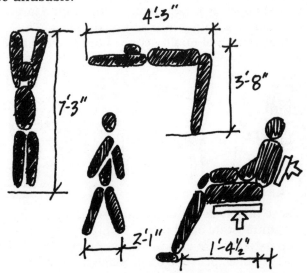

■ In your design, then, you need to make sure the environment fits the person. A dining table needs to be the right height, or those eating at it won't enjoy their meal. The back of a chair needs to be the right shape and size, or the user won't be comfortable. A bathroom will ideally have adequate width to allow the user to dry his or her back with a towel. A filing cabinet needs to have drawers of a particular depth, and needs to stand at a certain height, in order to be of greatest utility to the secretary who will be using it.

SPACIAL INTERFACE ACTION/REACTION

■ The next factor to keep in mind as you design to human scale is the interface between the human body and the spaces around it. Consider a church. If the church has high ceilings you get a feeling of awe and reverence as soon as you enter the doors. The bench you kneel on, the pulpit you stand at, and the pew you sit on all have different functions and all create different feelings within you. I'm not only talking about the *use* you put those interior elements to, though that's important. But in addition the actual placement of those elements in the room has an effect. *The design itself will influence how the person reacts to the interior you're working with.* The human-space interface determines how the person is acted upon by his environment, and how that person reacts to it.

HUMAN RELATIONSHIP DISTANCE

■ Another human-scale element is the distance at which two people relate to one another. Each person has his own territory, a distance around himself that he likes to keep. That distance is called personal space, and we always have it, though it changes with the circumstances.

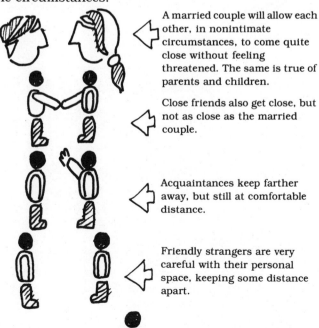

A married couple will allow each other, in nonintimate circumstances, to come quite close without feeling threatened. The same is true of parents and children.

Close friends also get close, but not as close as the married couple.

Acquaintances keep farther away, but still at comfortable distance.

Friendly strangers are very careful with their personal space, keeping some distance apart.

Enemies stay a good distance away from each other—when they're together at all!

HIERARCHY OF SPACE

■ The final element of human scale is spatial hierarchy. No design is static; instead it's dynamic, always moving. People have different needs at different times about their usage of space.

■ The designer deals with this problem by using various levels of space. Each segment of a particular building has a different function and fits into a different part of the leveled hierarchy. For example, when you approach an office, you're walking on the public sidewalk. That's neutral space. Then you enter the doorway, the first segment of the interior hierarchy. Its function, of course, is to allow entry to the building. Next, you may find yourself in a hallway. Its function is to direct you through the building. You go to a particular suite of offices through another doorway. You find yourself in a lobby. It's been put there to help you get your bearings on the office as a whole, and to provide a space where people can wait or meet one another. You approach the secretary who sits at the back of the lobby area. The office space is not set off by walls, but it's there nonetheless. And now you're moving into a particular person's space.

■ The same is true of a home. There are public places in a home, semi-public places, and private places.

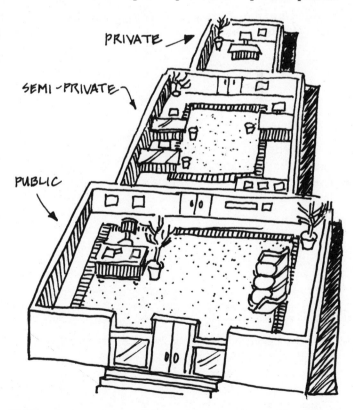

■ The designer must take care to arrange each part of a building according to its function, according to its place in the hierarchy. If he does, he'll have a successful design, one that meets the need.

FURNITURE

- Furniture is a vital element of interior design. It acts both as an item of utility and as one of aesthetics. Without furniture the room would lose much of its usefulness; the designer must therefore carefully consider the furniture that he includes in his design.

- Beauty and function must both be part of the plan. If the designer sacrifices the beauty strictly for the function, he is eliminating a part of the design that is important to the interior's inhabitants. The human psyche responds to the aesthetics of design nearly as much as to its usability; comfort often flows from appearance. If, on the other hand, the designer sacrifices function for beauty, again he is neglecting a crucial part of the design. The result in either case is a failed design.

Folding Chairs

Chairs that collapse for easy storage

Desk Chairs

Chairs made for sitting at desks and tables, often featuring castors for increased mobility, also having construction that accommodates long-term seating

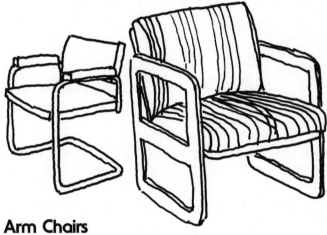

Arm Chairs

Chairs with arm-rests

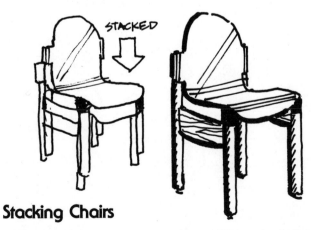

Stacking Chairs

Chairs that can be placed on top of one another to maximize use of limited storage space

Side Chairs

Chairs without arm-rests

Lounge Chairs

Heavy, high-backed, upholstered arm chairs

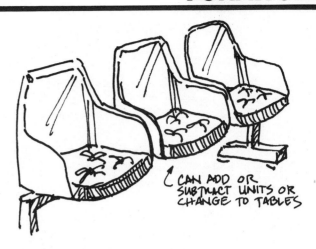

CAN ADD OR SUBTRACT UNITS OR CHANGE TO TABLES

Gang Seating

Interconnected seats or chairs found in such places as airports, doctors' offices, auditoriums, etc.

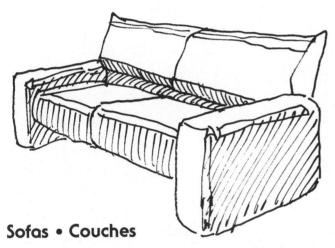

Sofas • Couches

Long, upholstered seating with arms and back

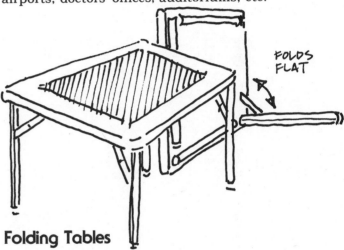

FOLDS FLAT

Folding Tables

Tables with either collapsible legs or top, designed to facilitate storage in limited space

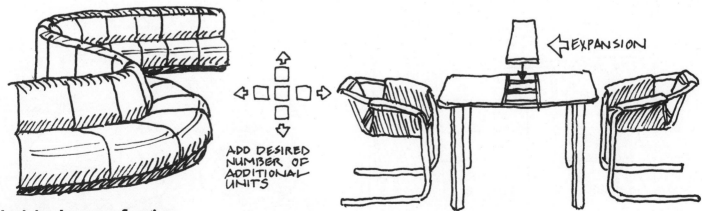

ADD DESIRED NUMBER OF ADDITIONAL UNITS

EXPANSION

Modular Lounge Seating

Multi-unit bench and chair components that fit together (not necessarily interlocking), and that can be arranged to accommodate various spaces and contours; a favorite for public spaces

Dining Table

Used for serving and consuming meals; often designed with additional leaves in order to accommodate various group sizes

FURNITURE

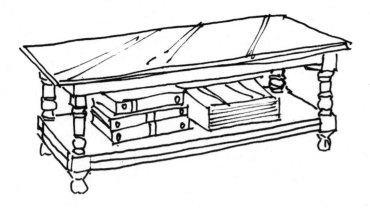

Coffee Table

Low-cut elongated table, usually no higher than the seat of a chair; generally found in the living area of a home, near or in front of the sofa

CREATED IMAGE...
AN IMPORTANT FACTOR

Executive Desk

A larger desk usually associated with business and corporate offices

USUALLY NEXT TO SOFA OR ARMCHAIR

Side or End Table

A small table, usually about the height of the arm of a chair and used beside a larger piece of furniture

Home or Secretary Desk

A smaller desk suited for home use and often used in businesses

Desk

A piece of furniture that has a suitable writing surface as well as a number of drawers and/or compartments for storage of papers, writing utensils, etc.

Conference Table

A large table used especially for gatherings of business associates; designed to facilitate interaction

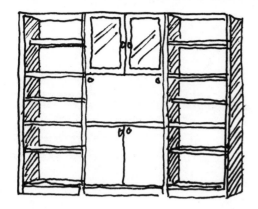

Modular Storage

A system of individual and oftentimes interconnecting compartments, shelves, or cabinets that can be added on to, taken down, or rearranged as space allows; used to maximize space and efficiency

FLEXIBLE

Room Dividers

Free-standing panels used to subdivide a large room into smaller, more private spaces; can be made of wood, bamboo, or fabric

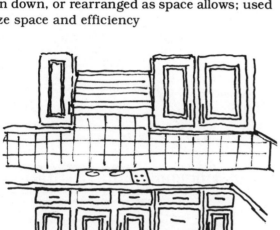

Cabinets

Cases and/or cupboards usually having doors and shelves

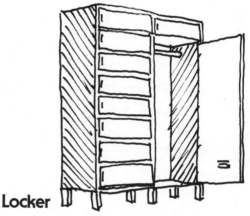

Locker

A chest, drawer, cupboard, or other storage compartment that is made to be locked

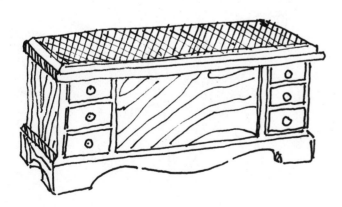

Drawers, Vanities, and Chests

Self-contained storage units, usually used in the home

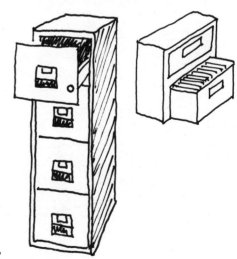

Filing Cabinet

A cabinet with drawers used to keep papers and records in order; generally associated with business offices

FURNITURE

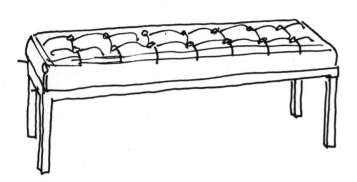

Bench

A long seat without arms or back

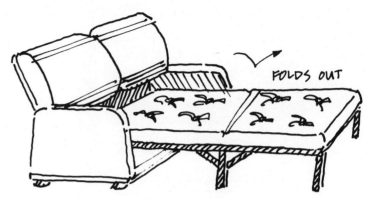

Sofa Bed

A dual-use piece of furniture that can be converted from a sofa to a bed

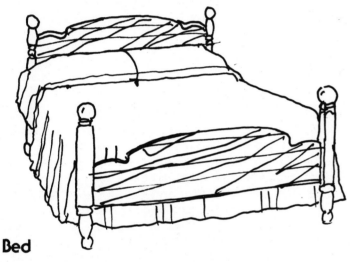

Bed

A piece of furniture used for sleeping: King size—72" x 84"; Queen size—60" x 80"; Full or double bed—54" x 75"; Twin or single bed—39" x 75"

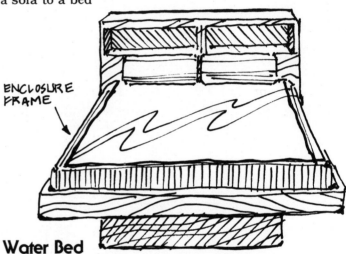

Water Bed

A bed with a plastic, water-filled mattress, usually requiring a stronger support frame and such special accessories as a heater, liner, etc.

Bunk Bed

Twin beds stacked vertically to maximize limited space

Outdoor Patio Furniture

Mobile, weather-resistant furniture usually made with aluminum or redwood frames

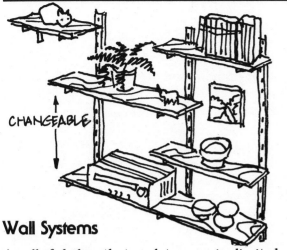

Wall Systems

A wall of shelves that work to organize limited space in a maximum way

High Tech

High tech stands for *high technology.* High tech furniture is furniture that is designed from industrial hardware but is used in the office or home environment. Examples of that hardware include shelving, scaffolding, PVC tubing, and so forth.

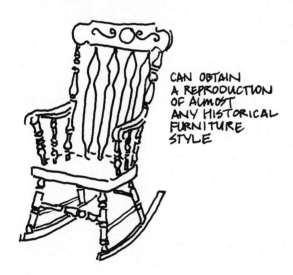

CAN OBTAIN A REPRODUCTION OF ALMOST ANY HISTORICAL FURNITURE STYLE

Period

There are two forms of period furniture. The first is the true antique. This category of furniture is often difficult to find—and invariably costs more than the actual usability of the piece justifies. Antique furniture is really *apropos* only for collectors.

The second form of period furniture is newly constructed pieces but it uses the designs of the period in question. For instance, a manufacturer today may make a replica of a Loius XIV chair.

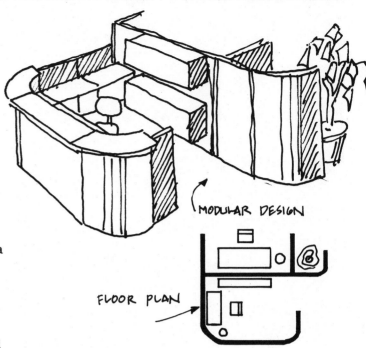

MODULAR DESIGN

FLOOR PLAN

Office Landscape

This is a relatively new approach to office design. Office landscape works on the theory that communication patterns are more important to the efficient functioning of an office than are such things as appearance, status of the workers, or tradition. Communication in the office landscape design is greatly enhanced by the absence of walls and partitions. People who must have frequent contact are placed close together. Spaces that provide for communication flow are shared, rather than repeated from room to room.

The greatest disadvantages of sharing space are noise and lack of privacy. The noise problem is handled by completely carpeting the floors and having acoustically effective ceilings. Heavy furniture with solid surfaces is avoided, because it reflects and sometimes amplifies sound. Noisy office machines are moved to another part of the building, as are permanent files.

The need for privacy is handled by using a nongeometric approach to the design. Care is taken that no two workers are placed facing each other. Furniture, screens, and storage units are placed to give each worker the feeling of private space, without hindering the communication flow.

Office landscape has been successfully used in Germany, Scandinavia, and England. Workers have been pleased with their work environments in office landscaped buildings; and the owners of the buildings have been impressed with the great cost savings they've experienced. Office landscape should be considered as one alternative in the design of the effective office.

LIGHTING

■ Over 85 percent of all we experience in life comes to us through the sense of sight. Sight is critical to our survival in and enjoyment of our environment. The most important element of interior design is form, both of the room and of the elements within it. The sense of sight plays the major role in the interpretation of form. Without light there is no sight.

KINDS OF LIGHTING

■ There are commonly only three kinds of lighting used in interior design:

FLUORESCENT LAMP

BALLAST

1 Fluorescent lighting, the light given off by the electrical stimulation of gas, is an even, white light.

INCANDESCENT LAMP

2 Incandescent light, the light given off by the electrical stimulation of a metal filament, is a softer, yellower light.

3 Natural lighting is received through skylights and windows. The effectiveness and usability of natural lighting vary greatly depending on the season, the time of day, the size and shape and relative position of the windows, and other factors such as curtains.

IMPORTANT RATIOS

- $\dfrac{\text{BALLAST EFFICIENCY}}{} = \dfrac{\text{WATTS OUT}}{\text{WATTS IN}}$

- $\dfrac{\text{LUMINOUS EFFICIENCY}}{} = \dfrac{\text{LAMP LUMENS}}{\text{LAMP WATTS}}$

- $\dfrac{\text{LUMINAIRE EFFICIENCY}}{} = \dfrac{\text{LUMENS EMITTED}}{\text{LUMENS GENERATED}}$

- $\dfrac{\text{COEFFICIENT OF UTILIZATION}}{} = \dfrac{\text{LUMENS REACHING WORK PLANE}}{\text{LUMENS EMITTED FROM LAMP}}$

USES FOR LIGHTING

■ There are two basic usages for lighting:

1. GENERAL Includes ceiling lighting, cove lighting, and perimeter lighting; also hanging, recessed, or wall fixtures.

2. LOCAL OR TASK LIGHTING
Usually provided by portable, hanging, directional, or table lamps. The key factors on task lighting are the amount and location of light on the work surface.

TASK LIGHTING

WORK SURFACE

■ The well-balanced room will usually have both kinds of lighting. Lamps are usually needed next to chairs for reading and other such tasks. Floor and table lamps are generally adequate for this purpose. Accent lighting is used to provide a dramatic touch to the room. It is used to light plants, works of art, bookshelves, and other displays. Track lights are useful for accent lighting. Kitchens and other work areas should have a good overall level of illumination. A luminous ceiling (ceiling fixtures) provides shadowless general lighting that's excellent for such rooms. Because of its illumination level, natural lighting should be used to light work areas whenever possible.

THE EFFECT OF LIGHT

■ The amount and quality of light can have profound effects on people:

Light can affect emotion or mood.

Light can affect productivity.

Light can affect awareness.

Light is often the element most neglected in interior design.

MODIFIERS OF LIGHT

■ Certain elements modify light—artificially or naturally—within the interior space.

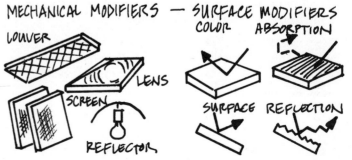

MECHANICAL MODIFIERS — SURFACE MODIFIERS
COLOR   ABSORPTION

LOUVER

LENS

SCREEN

REFLECTOR

SURFACE   REFLECTION

KINDS OF LIGHTS POSSIBLE WITHIN THE INTERIOR ENVIRONMENT

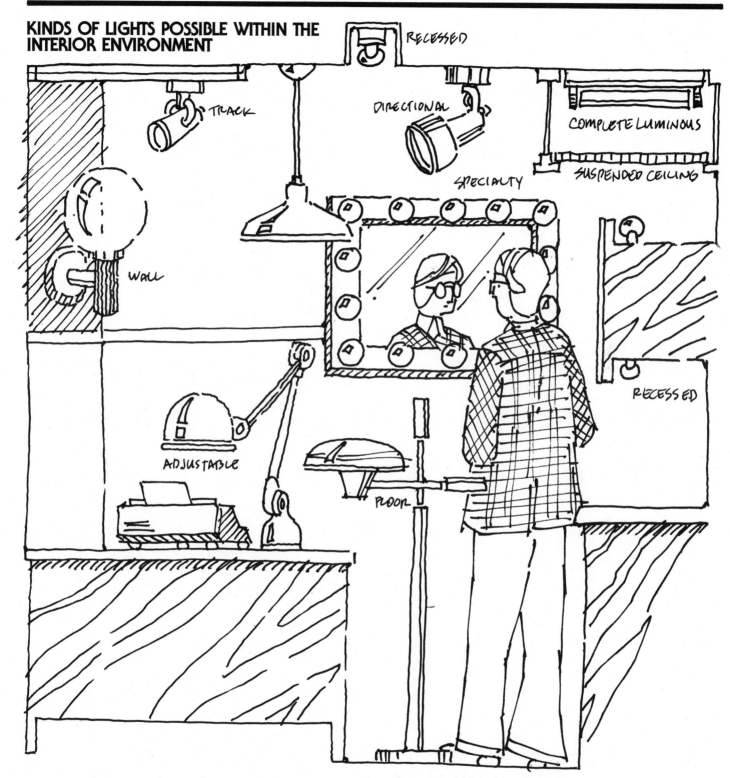

RECESSED

TRACK

DIRECTIONAL

COMPLETE LUMINOUS

SUSPENDED CEILING

SPECIALTY

WALL

RECESSED

ADJUSTABLE

FLOOR

MEASUREMENT OF ILLUMINATION

■ The level of illumination is measured in footcandles. A footcandle is the direct light on a surface one foot from a standardized candle.

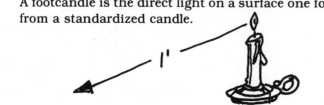

1'

RECOMMENDED LEVELS OF LIGHT

Area	Footcandles
ART GALLERIES	30-100
AUDITORIUMS	15
BANKS	150
CHURCHES	15-30
HOMES	70
HOSPITALS	2500
HOTELS	10-30
OFFICES	100

ACCESSORIES

- In every design you'll have certain elements that are of primary importance. Supporting those are items that are of secondary importance, but are nevertheless aesthetically or functionally necessary for that design. Those support items are called accessories.

- You'll note that accessories can be functional as well as aesthetic. The ideal, of course, is to have something that's decorative and useful at the same time.

PURPOSE OF ACCESSORIES

- Without accessories, a room is sterile. An interior needs to be more than just walls, floor, and ceiling. People are collectors of furniture and other things, and a room should reflect that. If your design comprises only bare walls or bare floor, with only the basic furniture, you should reconsider. There's much more that can be done. The purpose of accessories, then, in addition to their basic function, is to dress the room. It will make the interior finished—and livable.

- Accessories can be used in creating a visual center of interest, as with a throw rug or a picture. They can help you arrange other elements. They can help create a feeling of greater height in the room, or a lower ceiling, or whatever you choose, just by arranging them carefully and thoughtfully.

KEY POINTS ON ACCESSORIES

OVERLOAD Beware of the temptation to show too much in the room, to overload the senses. This is the first and most important caution you should keep in mind.

SUITABILITY Although the selection of accessories is unlimited, only a certain portion will be appropriate for your design. Use only accessories that are suited in form, style, and color to the rest of the design.

SELECTION You won't be able to use whatever accessories are near at hand. To meet the requirement of suitability, you'll need to spend time and have patience and discrimination in your selection.

CENTRAL CONCEPT Choose a central feeling, mood, or emotion that you want to create in the room and tie the accessories in to it.

HARMONY Strive for a proper balanced relationship within the room. You'll be much more able to achieve harmony if you've established your central concept. Relate all parts of the room—including accessories—to one another through color, texture, style, and material. The goal is *spatial continuity*.

CHANGEABILITY In your use of accessories, allow for at least some movement and change. Living environments are never static, and should never be designed that way.

PERSONALITY Accessories allow the user of the rooms to show his personal imprint. They allow him to make the room part of himself. (He's going to do it anyway—you might as well let him have an influence on what the room's accessories will be from the very beginning.)

SENTIMENTALITY The client may wish to place certain items of sentimental value in the interior. Such items can generally not be judged on an aesthetic basis; they must be included regardless of their intrinsic design value. If your client wishes to include sentimental items that lack artistic value, try to place them in an inconspicuous spot.

- Here are a few of the most common things used as accessories:

CLOCKS

Clocks are both uilitarian and aesthetic. They can be a very attractive and functional accessory.

OFFICE ACCESSORIES

- Office, restaurant, and lounge accessories are necessarily different from those found in residences, since the functions of such places are different.

PLANTS AND FOLIAGE

Plants are a popular means of accenting a room. They have an inherent beauty and add a warm, natural tone to even the most severe settings. Using a plant as an accessory gives you the opportunity to share your space with another living thing.

Plants must be located where the environmental conditions suit their growth.

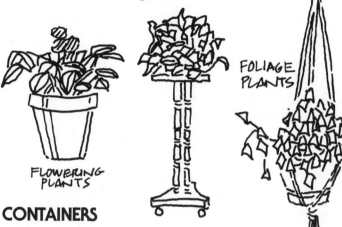

FLOWERING PLANTS

FOLIAGE PLANTS

CONTAINERS

Containers can serve both for storage and for decoration. They include things as diverse as ashtrays and pots and pans and baskets, as varied as facial tissue boxes and kitchen canisters. They can contain almost anything from plants to pasta, from matches to macadamia nuts.

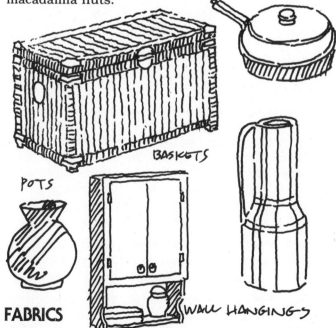

BASKETS

POTS

WALL HANGINGS

FABRICS

Fabrics soften edges and humanize our environment. They perform such functions as controlling light that comes through windows, absorbing noise, and insulating against heat and cold. Fabrics are unique in their place in interior design because they relate the furniture we sit on to the clothing we wear. They relate the carpet to the curtains, and the curtains to the tablecloth in the dining room. Bedding, linens, and other kinds of fabrics all function as accessories; they enrich the room, matching form to function.

ART AND DECORATIVE OBJECTS

These can be the focal point of a room. Displayed on wall, shelf, floor, or counter, they can add interest and beauty to an interior while they enrich it culturally as well.

OTHER ACCESSORIES

■ Other accessories you can consider in the design of a room include such things as awards, and trophies; magazines, books, and records; toys; televisions, stereos, home computers, and other kinds of electronic equipment; telephones; various kinds of dispensers; tools, equipment, and the like. Meaningful collections or hobbies can be prominently displayed on a shelf or wall, giving the room warmth and personality. Rocks, ceramics, mirrors, glassware, and seashells can all be used to spice up interior space. But care should be taken not to include accessories simply to fill up space. Clutter is too often the end result.

■ In sum, almost anything can work as an accessory!

MATERIALS

- Materials are the elements that are used to create the environment. They fall into five major categories:

    ROCK, such as stone or clay;

    ORGANIC, such as wood;

    METAL, which comes in many natural as well as processed forms;

    SYNTHETIC, such as glass or plastics;

    HYBRID, a combinaton of two or more of the above materials.

- These five elements are used in one form or another to create every kind of design imaginable. In this section I'll show how the basic materials are used to create floors, ceilings, walls, windows, doors, and hardware.

FLOORS

- There are two kinds of flooring, soft flooring such as carpet and hard flooring such as linoleum.

SOFT FLOORING comes in two forms: carpets and rugs. A carpet is designed to cover the entire floor; a rug covers only a portion of the floor. With the almost infinite variety of colors, textures, and patterns available, you can alter the room's apparent size and proportions by choosing the right flooring.

CARPETS There are five basic kinds of carpet construction: tufting, woven, needle-punch, knitted, and flocked. Ninety percent of all carpet made today is made with the tufting method. The needle-punch method is generally used with indoor-outdoor carpet. In selecting a carpet, look carefully at its construction. Bend the sample back to see how densely the fibers stick together. The less backing you can see, the better; that indicates the carpet is denser and will thus wear longer. Deeper pile carpet also will wear longer, since it has more yarn to wear away.

- There are a host of fibers that have been used in carpets, but five are superior to others in terms of beauty and cost-effectiveness:

- Wool—This is the luxury fiber, and all other fibers are compared to wool. It is also the fiber that costs the most, however.

- Nylon—Most carpets are made of nylon. When blended with wool (70 percent wool, 30 percent nylon) it retains many of wool's good qualities but costs less.

- Acrylic—Acrylics are next to nylons in terms of quantity produced. They wear well and compare favorably with wool in appearance.

- Polyester—This fiber also wears well. It combines the bulk of wool with the durability of nylon.

- Olefin—This fiber was introduced in the 1960s. It is used particularly in indoor-outdoor carpets.

STYLE CHARACTERISTICS

- In choosing a carpet there are several characteristics of surface style you should consider.

- Plain-textured carpets are even in texture and wear well.

- Tweed carpets are looped in a high-low pile and are usually most appropriate for formal rooms.

- Plush carpets are thick and luxurious and are most appropriate for formal rooms.

- Tone-on-tone carpets combine two or more tones of the same hue. It wears well under spotting.

- Embossed carpets have a combination high-low pile. It is extremely versatile and very popular.

- Sculptured carpets have a pattern on their surface. They are generally made of wool, are often custom-made, and are usually quite expensive.

- Shag rugs are sturdy and require little upkeep. They are generally made of nylon and polyester. Shag rugs go well in almost any environment and are very popular.

CARPET

PAD

TACKLESS

- Several types of underlays are available on the market. The underlay will improve the cushioning effect of the carpet, improve the carpet's noise absorption, and prolong the life of the carpet by as much as 75 percent. The most practical underlays are foam made of prime or bonded urethane and foam rubber. About 20 percent of the carpeting available already has the underlay attached.

RUGS The selection principles that apply to carpets are also valid for rugs. The function of the rug, however, will have a great bearing on what you choose.

- Art rugs are usually handcrafted. Their function is generally to serve as an aesthetic element in the room, rather than a practical one, and they should be placed accordingly.

- Area rugs are generally used to define a certain part of a room. The rug should be large enough to accommodate the groupings of furniture to be used in the room. Area rugs are very versatile and can often be moved from room to room or from place to place within a room.

HARD FLOORING Carpeting has become increasingly popular in recent years, but, interestingly, hard flooring is also very much in demand. Hard flooring is often so durable that it can flow from an inside hall to an outside porch or patio. Some floors require very little upkeep; and many hard floors have a natural beauty that carpeting cannot match.

Hard flooring comes in three general categories: resilient, nonresilient, and wood.

RESILIENT The most common form of resilient hard flooring is vinyl. Resilient flooring is extremely durable, and has traditionally been used in kitchens, bathrooms, and utility rooms. But with advances in technology it can be found in nearly any room in the house. Vinyl can be made to look like rich wood or marble, and with a cushion back it can be as comfortable as carpet.

Here are the basic kinds of resilient hard flooring:

- Asphalt Tile
- Cork Tile
- Cushion-Backed Vinyl
- Leather Tile
- Linoleum
- Rubber Tile
- Sheet Vinyl
- Vinyl Asbestos
- Vinyl Cork
- Vinyl Tile

NONRESILIENT The designer who chooses to use this kind of flooring has a world of options open to him. Here is a list of the kinds of nonresilient materials he can consider:

- Brick
- Ceramic Tile
- Concrete Tile
- Flagstone
- Glass Brick
- Marble
- Mexican Tile
- Pebble Tile
- Poured Seamless Vinyl
- Quarry Tile
- Slate
- Terrazzo

WOOD is the most popular and most versatile of all floor materials. It combines the beauty and warmth of a natural material with resilience and durability. It is easy to obtain, comes at a reasonable cost, and is easy to install.

Wood for flooring comes in several forms:

- Strips, with tongue and groove;
- Planks;
- Parquetry, which combines short pieces in various designs, assembled at the factory;
- Prefabricated squares;
- Wood veneer, which is backed wih aluminum, asbestos, and vinyl, and which is topped with a surface of vinyl sheeting.

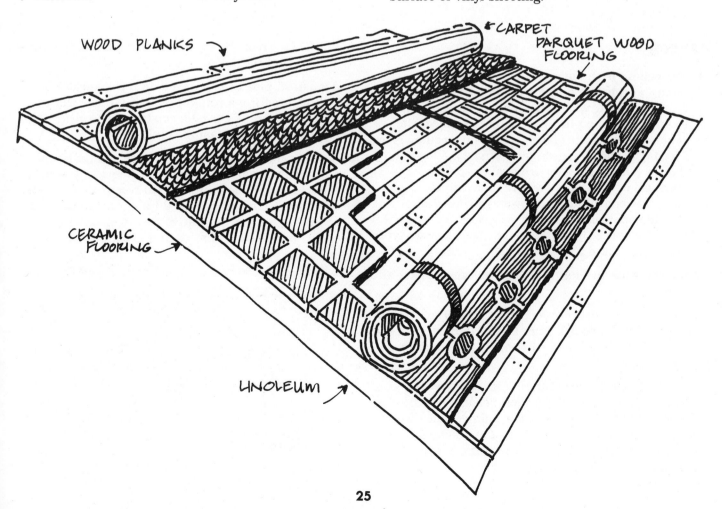

WOOD PLANKS

CARPET

PARQUET WOOD FLOORING

CERAMIC FLOORING

LINOLEUM

MATERIALS

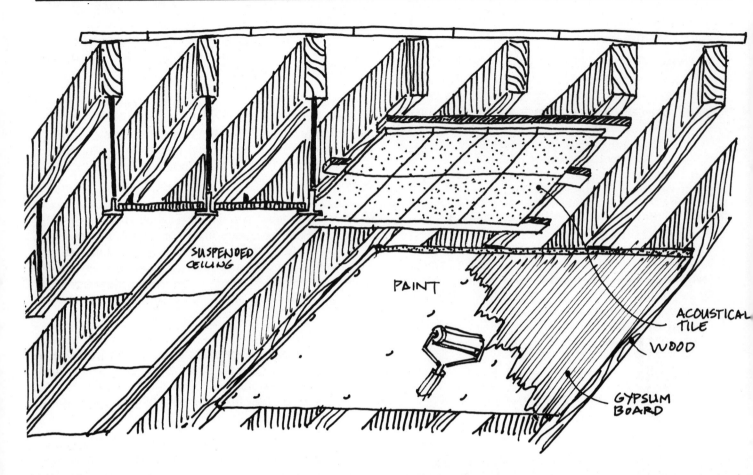

SUSPENDED CEILING

PAINT

ACOUSTICAL TILE

WOOD

GYPSUM BOARD

CEILINGS

■ The ceiling is the most neglected area of the room—and is one of the most important. How you treat the ceiling will determine how large or small the room feels, which in turn can greatly affect the general atmosphere of the room. A high ceiling gives a feeling of spaciousness and formality. A low ceiling creates a more cozy, informal atmosphere. Light-colored ceilings seem higher, while dark-colored ceilings feel lower. In your design you should consider the ceiling very carefully, so that it will achieve the effect you desire. There are two types of ceilings: hard and acoustical.

HARD There are two kinds of hard ceilings; plaster and wood.

● Plaster is the most common ceiling material, often in the form of wallboard. Once installed or applied, the plaster can be finished with either a smooth or a textured surface.

● Wood is generally used in ceilings only to achieve a rustic or period effect. Wooden beams give personality and character to a ceiling. Some wood beams are hand-hewn, but most are factory made. The beams can be painted or left plain, depending on the feeling you hope to achieve.

ACOUSTICAL There are two kinds of acoustical ceilings; plaster and tile.

● Acoustical plaster is sprayed onto the surface of the ceiling, creating a rough-textured surface that absorbs noise. The plaster can be used to good effect, achieving a very pleasing result.

● Acoustical tile is very popular, especially in kitchens and family rooms. It is also very frequently seen in schools and office buildings. In recent years it has improved from the standard functional appearance, achieving a more decorative feel. Acoustical tile comes in a variety of sizes and is easy to install.

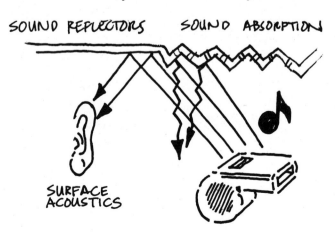

SOUND REFLECTORS   SOUND ABSORPTION

SURFACE ACOUSTICS

PAINT   WALLPAPER   TILE

GYPSUM BOARD

WALL PANELING

2X4 STUD WALL

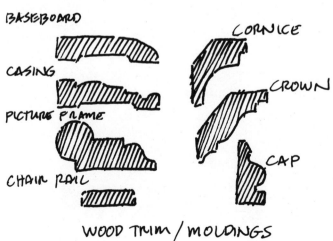

BASEBOARD

CASING

PICTURE FRAME

CHAIR RAIL

CORNICE

CROWN

CAP

WOOD TRIM / MOLDINGS

WALLS

■ The walls are without dispute the most important background elements in a room, partly because they occupy the greatest space. In addition to aesthetic purposes, the walls also perform several other vital functions. They serve as dividers of the larger interior space. They house such building components as plumbing, electrical wiring, and insulation.

■ Just as with ceilings and floors, the choice of wall material will have a major bearing on the atmosphere of the room. Dark wood will give the room a warm feel, but will make it feel smaller. Stone will give a cool, rustic feel, but one of strength, durability, security. Plaster is the most common wall material, both because of its great versatility with different room elements and because of its relatively low cost.

■ In the design of your room, you should choose your wall coverings carefully, considering the atmosphere the covering will give, as well as its durability and unity with the entirety of the room. I've divided the wall coverings available into three basic kinds: rigid, nonrigid, and paint.

RIGID WALL COVERINGS are generally very strong and durable. They range in price from the very expensive to the quite inexpensive. There are basically two kinds of rigid wall coverings: masonry, and paneling. An adjunct to the rigid type of wall covering is wood trim, or molding.

Here are the kinds of masonry you can consider:
- Brick
- Cement and Cinder Block
- Ceramic Tile
- Glass Block
- Metal Tile
- Plaster and Stucco
- Stone

Here are the kinds of paneling:
- Fiberglass Panels
- Wallboard (Plasterboard)
- Hardboard Wallboard (Pressed Wood)
- Plastic Laminate Wallboard
- Plywood
- Solid Wood

NONRIGID WALL COVERINGS A definitely viable alternative to rigid wall coverings is the nonrigid or flexible type. There is a great variety to choose from, and with creative thought you can often find the solution to your design problem in one of the many forms of nonrigid wall coverings presently on the market.

MATERIALS

■ The nonrigid wall coverings you can consider are these:

- Carpet
- Cork
- Fabric
- Leather Tile
- Vinyl Paper
- Wallpaper

PAINT This is the most popular of all wall coverings, being used perhaps as much as all other kinds combined. It is extremely versatile and easy to use. Perhaps the *most* usable is the water-thinned latex paint. In terms of muss and fuss, it's a dream to apply; and it can be obtained in varying degrees of flatness or glossiness.

■ Even though we have paint under the wall-covering category, it's so versatile that it can be used on ceilings and floors as well.

■ Here are the many kinds of paints available. In addition to the types listed are various sealers and undercoats that help prepare the surface for the paint but that are not seen as part of the final design of the interior. There are also many exterior paints on the market, but this list only notes the primary interior paints:

- Alkyd Flat Paint
- Alkyd Gloss Enamel
- Alkyd Semi-Gloss
- Aluminum Paint
- Catalyzed Enamel
- Cement-Base Paint
- Clear Polyurethane
- Floor Enamel
- Floor Varnish
- Interior Varnish
- Latex Flat Paint
- Latex Semi-Gloss
- Rubber-Base Paint
- Shellac
- Stain

WINDOW TREATMENTS

GLASS: SOLID COLORED BEVELED MULTI-PANED MULTIPLE MULLIONS LEADED STAINED

SHUTTERS

CURTAINS

FULL LENGTH

BLINDS

WINDOWS are placed in buildings primarily to let in light and air, and they should be designed accordingly. Not too many years ago architects created only standard casement-type windows. But now there are many more options.

■ The window may be a large picture-type window; or it may be several panes of glass in horizontal lines. A room may have asymmetrical windows, corner windows, or a two-story window.

■ A window is an important focal point in a room, and how it is designed will have a bearing on how a person reacts to the room as a whole. The framing of the window is an important element to consider. It can be framed in wood, metal, or even vinyl. The designer can choose to have a large, single pane, or to divide it with mullions.

■ The glass itself will probably be clear, though it need not be. Other options are translucent glass, colored glass, and stained glass. Your choice will determine the atmosphere of the room.

■ Often the most options are available in choosing window coverings. Here are the most common coverings, or dressings:

- Drapery or Curtains
- Grillwork Screens
- Louvered Shutters
- Matchstick Bamboo Blinds
- Sheer, or Glass, Curtains
- Shoji Screens
- Venetian Blinds
- Vinyl Window Shades

DOORS can be made an interesting element in the room. A game room door, for instance, can be given bright, exciting colors to match the feeling desired in the room. A formal room can be given a heavier wooden door. An outside door can have windows for visual interest and greater depth, or can be made of metal for increased security. Existing doors can be altered through the judicious use of molding, wood blocks, or wall covering.

■ Types of doors you can consider, depending on the requirements of the room, include:

- Accordion Door
- Bamboo Blinds
- Dutch Door
- Flush Door
- Folding Door
- French Door
- Hollow-Core Door
- Louvered Door
- Panel Door
- Sliding Door

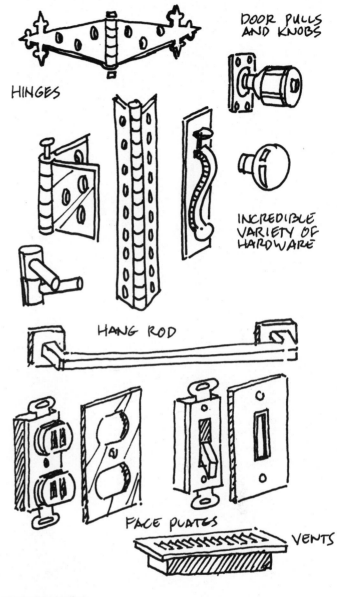

HARDWARE

■ Every interior has a certain amount of hardware that should be considered as part of the overall design. If you are careful in your selection of the hardware, you'll enhance rather than detract from the overall feel of the room.

■ Here are some of the kinds of hardware you should keep in mind:

- Curtain Rods
- Door Knobs
- Door Locks
- Cabinet Knobs
- Cabinet Latches
- Window Latches
- Light Switches
- Electrical Plug-ins
- Water Faucets
- Towel Racks
- Soap Dishes
- Toilet Tissue Holders
- Fuse or Circuit-Breaker Boxes
- Telephone Jacks
- Furnace and Air Conditioner Vents
- Stairway Railings
- And so on!

COLOR

NO COLOR WITHOUT LIGHT

■ We get color from light. If there were no light there would be no color—but where light is present, color is always present also. In dealing with color, then, the interior designer must also remember to deal with light. There are two ways light can cause us to see color: either by reflecting off the surface of an object, or by being absorbed into that surface. (See lighting section.)

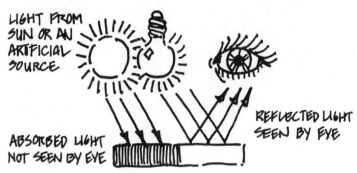

LIGHT FROM SUN OR AN ARTIFICIAL SOURCE

REFLECTED LIGHT SEEN BY EYE

ABSORBED LIGHT NOT SEEN BY EYE

■ Color comes in three dimensions: hue, value, and intensity.

1. **HUE** is the name of the color. It indicates how the color relates to other colors. It is the hue that distinguishes one color from another. Even though there are thousands of hues, the typical person knows the names of only fifteen or twenty. We remember the names of those that are the most obvious, but color and color relationships exist in enormous variety.

WARM HUES ADVANCE

COOL HUES RECEDE

Hues can be used to alter the apparent size and proportions of a room or object.

2. **VALUE** is the word used to indicate the lightness or darkness of a particular color. A color's value should also be considered in making a color choice. If you want a room to look smaller, you should choose a color that has a darker value. But if you want to give the illusion that the room is larger, use the lighter value. To make a color lighter or darker, start with a pure hue and then add white or black.

LIGHT VALUES EXPAND

HEAVY VALUES RECEDE

3. **INTENSITY** indicates how pure and strong a particular hue is. It is the intensity that gives a feeling of brightness or dullness in a color. Hues that are purer, that have more intensity, generally are better choices in design.

WARM COLOR DARK VALUE

COOL COLOR LIGHT VALUE

CONTRACTS

EXPANDS

COLOR IS AFFECTED BY ITS ENVIRONMENT

■ In dealing with color you need to be conscious of the context the color will be placed in. How well a color "works" will depend on its environment. In any environment, each color affects all other colors. Each hue, value, and intensity changes as it is coupled with others. Remember that the color won't retain its purity when it moves into the environment of the interior you're designing. Remember also that different kinds of lighting (fluorescent, incandescent, natural) and different levels of lighting will change the appearance of a given color.

■ Color also changes because of the surface the color is applied on. A hue on a hard, smooth surface will appear glossy. On a more absorbent surface that same hue will have a duller appearance. The kind of surface you're working on will determine how the viewer will respond to the color you select.

■ If you want to see how a particular color really looks, take a look at it in an environment with elements, surfaces, lighting, etc., similar to those in the final context. Keep in mind the many variables that affect color: lighting, surface, texture, surrounding colors, and so forth.

COLOR

VALUE SURROUNDINGS

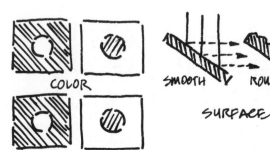

SMOOTH   ROUGH

SURFACE

COLOR AFFECTS ITS ENVIRONMENT

■ Color is crucial to good design. One of the things you want to do in your design is create an emotion in the viewer/user. Whether it's creativity or relaxation or productivity or general well-being, you want the user to *feel* something. Color is the most effective door to emotion in interior design.

Red—anger, excitement, heat, happiness, sex, eating

Green—nature, relaxation, summer, envy

White—purity, cleanliness, winter, day

Blue—royalty, water, coolness, sadness, receding

Yellow—autumn, cowardice, intensity, warmth, expansion

Black—depression, night, sleep

THE COLOR WHEEL

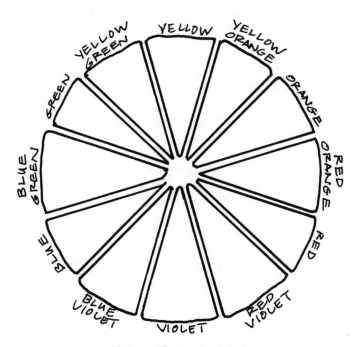

FULL COLOR WHEEL

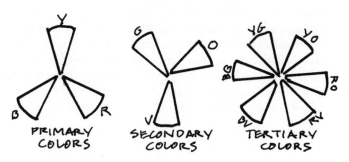

PRIMARY COLORS   SECONDARY COLORS   TERTIARY COLORS

COLOR SCHEMES

■ There are several kinds of color schemes or arrangements in popular usage. The most widely used are the **COMPLEMENTARY** schemes, which provide more variety than other arrangements. There are many different variations of complementary schemes; all use colors of contrasting hues. A combination of contrasting hues makes both hues more attractive. If their intensity is the same, the complement of colors will make both feel even more intense, which may or may not be desirable. Complementary schemes invariably mix warm colors (yellow, orange, red) with cool colors (violet, blue, green). But there must be one hue in particular that is chosen to be dominant, if the design is to be pleasing and effective. Here are five types of complementary schemes:

1. **DIRECT COMPLEMENT** This uses two colors chosen from opposite sides of the color wheel. This scheme allows for heavy contrast.
2. **SPLIT COMPLEMENT** This uses three colors, any one hue, plus the two hues that are next to its complement (opposite). In this scheme, the colors provide less contrast than in the direct complement.
3. **TRIAD SCHEME** This also uses three colors, each equidistant from the next on the wheel. This scheme allows for either heavy or muted contrast.
4. **DOUBLE COMPLEMENT** This scheme uses four colors, two sets of complements. This doubles the combinations of color available.
5. **ALTERNATE COMPLEMENT** This four-color scheme combines the triad with the direct complement.

■ Another color arrangement designers often use is the **ANALOGOUS** scheme. This kind of scheme juxtaposes between three and six colors from the wheel—all from the same side of the wheel. Analogous schemes are easy on the eye, since they borrow from the natural state of the colors. These schemes usually have one color that's common to the scheme as a whole. To be used successfully, an analogous scheme must have one dominant color.

COLOR SELECTION

■ How do you select the right color for a particular design? Start by considering the uses of the design. What kind of color would serve them best? As you select, keep in mind the acceptable combinations of color that we've discussed. Use hues that appeal to your client at least as much as they do to you.

■ One source of information about the colors, patterns, and textures that will be effective in a client's environment is his/her wardrobe. The clothes exhibit past choices, and dominant decision patterns will always emerge.

SPACE

- Interior design uses space. Arranging and manipulating the forms, colors, patterns, and textures organized within the space are what a designer does.

SPACIAL BOUNDARIES

- Design is made up of the division of space. Space is usually divided by different kinds of boundaries. There is a boundary dividing outside from inside. There are boundaries that exist strictly on the outside, such as fences, hedges, shadows, and so forth. On the inside, dividing the space into self-contained units, are other kinds of boundaries: walls, ceilings, floors, room dividers, and so forth.

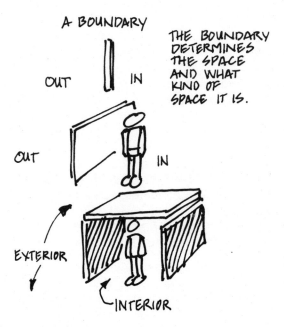

A BOUNDARY

OUT · IN

THE BOUNDARY DETERMINES THE SPACE AND WHAT KIND OF SPACE IT IS.

OUT · IN

EXTERIOR

INTERIOR

INTERIOR SPACE

- A designer's work is judged by how effectively he has been able to divide up and utilize the available space.

- Interior space is vitally important in our lives. We spend most of our time, from beginning to end, inside. We go to school indoors; we eat and sleep indoors; we generally work indoors. And the beauty of interior space is that it can be created and modified by man. We talk about the natural environment but most of us have little close contact with it. Our immediate world is man-made. Owing to resource scarcity and increasing population, *how* this world is made becomes crucial to our sanity and survival.

- There are basically four kinds of interior space: living space, work space, public space, and special-purpose space. Each has its own special demands and needs. Each is arranged and designed in a different way.

LIVING · WORK · PUBLIC

QUESTIONS

- To make certain that you're making the very best possible use of the interior's space, ask yourself these questions:

- What is the main thing the space will be used for?
- How does this space relate to other spaces in the building?
- What is the intended flow through the space?
- What is the intended flow through the building?
- Is the flow the same for people as for things?
- Does this space have any special requirements?
- What are the lighting needs of the space? Are they the same for daytime as for nighttime?
- Have the elements of heating, cooling, and acoustics been considered in the design of the space?
- Have all the secondary uses of the space, such as maintenance, been considered?
- Does the space create the right mood or feeling?
- Does the space have the proper "meaning" to the viewer/user?
- Have the proper materials been chosen for the development of the space? Are they the most economical while still being the most functional?
- Have budget constraints been respected in the design and development of the space?
- Have the client's special needs and desires been respected?
- Have the location and climate in which the space is located been given proper consideration?
- Does the designer have an overall intent, giving an overall unity to the space?

ANSWERS

- Interior design involves finding answers to questions. If there are no questions waiting to be answered then there is no design. Shallow, trite questions bring superficial design answers. It has been said that finding out what the questions are is much harder and more important than finding the answers. The answers to the questions above and to still other questions unique to a project determine more than anything else the design direction taken.

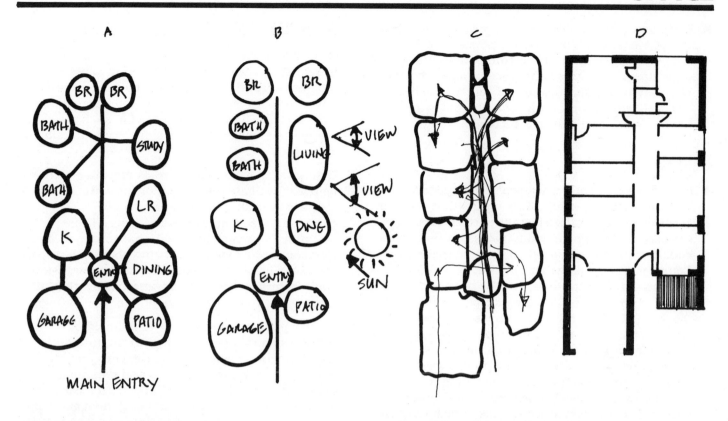

MAIN ENTRY

EVOLUTION OF SPACE

- No matter what the use of the space will be, the designer will take it through an evolution to get the desired results. His goal is to have the best positioning of the interior spaces in relation to the user. He will move from general principles and ideas to specific applications; he'll go from the rough sketch to the finished floor plan. His efforts to evolve his division of space will be some of the most important work he'll do within the profession, since the effective creation of space is the essence of interior design.

- Here are the steps the designer goes through as he evolves the space he has available:

1: **DEFINE** the segments of space needed within the whole. You can accomplish this with a diagram.

2: **DETERMINE** the best position or relationship of each space-segment. This involves seeing each space in its context. You'll undoubtedly do some arranging and rearranging to accomplish this step.

3: **DECIDE** on the best size and shape of each space. As you do this, keep in mind the activities that will be carried out in the space, as well as the furniture and other materials and elements that will be needed.

4: **TIGHTEN** up the design that's been created. Make a formal, complete drawing to make certain that the entire design works well as a unit, and to be sure that no details have been overlooked.

FLOW THROUGH SPACE

- Most buildings are in constant use—a fact the designer must never forget. A building or room will have constant incoming and outgoing traffic, continual flow across its boundaries.

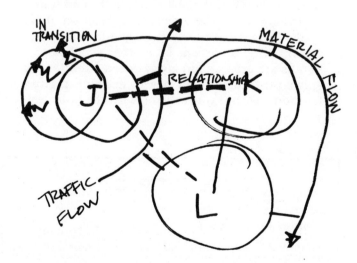

- These patterns of movement must be considered in the design of space. Material, information, people, control, light, air, energy—these are all elements that must be designed for. Keep them all in mind as you work out the best use of space for the particular interior you're concerned with. Design with the flow.

SOLUTIONS

- When you accept a design job you at the same time accept a problem. The problem is this: how do you meet the client's need, stay within budget, and at the same time create an aesthetically pleasing design? The answer to that question, of course, will decide how well your design works out. The following few critical points will help you succeed.

GESTALT

- A good place to start when you're looking for solutions is with *gestalt*. This means that you look at the whole rather than just the parts. It means that you can analyze the individual parts, but that, in the end, the whole is greater than the sum of the parts. Consider a painting as an example. You look at a landscape and notice how well the trees are rendered; you appreciate the nice paint quality in the water of the lake; you're impressed by the artist's use of value in the sky. But the painting isn't really enjoyable until you look at the thing as a whole. Then, suddenly, the whole thing *works* together. Here's another example. You're listening to a symphony. The melody line is nice, but rather simple. The percussion section has some interesting rhythms, but they're nothing to write home about. The woodwinds are weaving a counterpoint to the melody. All by itself, each element is nice, but nothing spectacular. Then you put it all together; you begin listening from the point of view of gestalt. Voilà! You've got a magnificent piece of music.

- Viewing the whole design at key stages in the design process gives you the ability to see the end from the beginning. You have a picture and can see the gradual refinement toward completion rather than getting hung up on one or another small part. Details are critical and always need attention, but only a continual overall view or gestalt can give you harmony, within yourself and with the final design.

THE GESTALT THEORY

1. **THE PARTS** of a design solution may be considered, analyzed, and evaluated as distinct components.

2. **THE WHOLE** of a design solution is different from and *greater* than the sum of its parts. Thus each of the two levels of designing, one the particular and one the general, is incomplete without the other.

HUMAN RESPONSE

- Response is the user's reaction to his environment. Response is always subjective and involves a value judgment. But the designer can have an influence on how the user responds. In fact, good design *means* that elements have been arranged in such a way that the user's potential response has been evaluated in advance.

- Determining what people are comfortable with will help you evaluate response. For instance, they aren't willing to carry on private conversations in nonprivate settings. Those designing offices should keep that in mind. Many elements come together to bring about the response the user will have. You should consider, for instance, such factors as lighting, vibration, acoustics, air circulation, room arrangement, etc.

- A particular response can be stimulated by conventionalized patterns within the interior environment. People perceive the cues and often react automatically in a social and psychological pattern. For example, one whispers in a cathedral. Knowing these patterns and using them can help a designer.

POINTS OF VIEW

- In order to determine a user's potential response, look at things from his point of view. Most designers consider points of view—but they don't consider them all. For instance, many buildings are constructed in such a way that maintenance is well nigh impossible. You can avoid such problems by looking at the point of view of *every* user of your design. Consider the following users of an office building as an example of how complete you ought to be.

  - Office workers
  - Cleaning people
  - Maintenance people (heating, cooling, water, plumbing, electricity, elevators, etc.)
  - Security workers
  - Parking attendants
  - Building supervisors
  - Vending-machine suppliers
  - Delivery persons
  - **Emergency service workers**
  - Visitors
  - Meter readers
  - Salesmen
  - Consultants
  - And any others you can think of

■ Time—5:30 Friday September 23

Dominant need: A soft chair to collapse in after work.

Subdominant need: To read the newspaper.

Subordinate need: Pleasing elements to enhance relaxation and security.

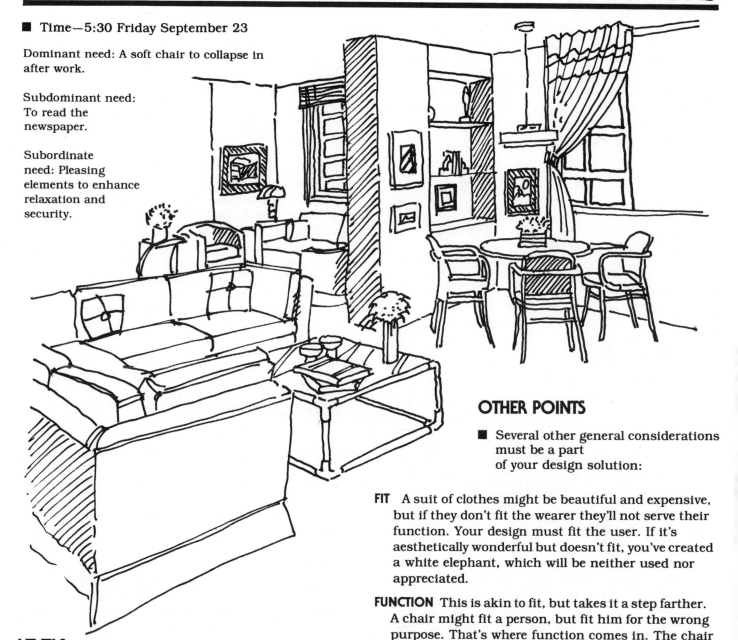

LEVELS

■ Design in the interior is multileveled. An interior serves not one function but many. These levels of use and need constantly change. A bedroom may be used and appreciated differently during the day and at night, etc.

DESIGN COMPROMISE

■ Compromise in design is inevitable. Certain areas in the design may create conflicts between needs or between people. When these conflicts become too many and too divergent you may have a flop on your hands. Design is best when few decision makers are involved. Committees are often destructive to cohesive design.

OTHER POINTS

■ Several other general considerations must be a part of your design solution:

FIT A suit of clothes might be beautiful and expensive, but if they don't fit the wearer they'll not serve their function. Your design must fit the user. If it's aesthetically wonderful but doesn't fit, you've created a white elephant, which will be neither used nor appreciated.

FUNCTION This is akin to fit, but takes it a step farther. A chair might fit a person, but fit him for the wrong purpose. That's where function comes in. The chair also must fit him for the specific job he needs to do.

ECOMONY Most design projects have a budget. Stay within it.

EMOTION Design must stimulate the appropriate response from its user. A funeral parlor probably shouldn't be decorated with gay colors, for instance; and tools have safety features that are designed to *look* safe, so the user can work with confidence.

MEANING Different designs mean different things. You can make a door look dignified, secure, flimsy, enticing, or uninteresting, all by how you design it. Each interior should have its own meaning, and you must let that meaning show in your design.

COMMUNICATION

■ Interior design is a visual profession. Most of its results are experienced and evaluated by the eyes. The design of a particular project may be a beautiful and effective solution, but if it can't be communicated it becomes irrelevant. The ability to communicate your design to yourself, client, and contractor is critical. There are 3 stages in the communication process:

STAGE 1:
DESIGN DEVELOPMENT

■ The purpose of design development is to help you *see* the solution to the problem. The key is the ability to visualize your ideas on paper. To be most effective, you should at first stress quantity over quality. Go for a good number of different kinds of solutions in a short period of time.

THUMBNAIL SKETCHES

ROUGH MODEL

ROUGH SKETCHES Your starting point should be the rough sketch. Get some thin tracing paper, the kind usually intended for the wastepaper basket, to work on. Your writing implements should be simple—a pencil, a black felt pen, and chalk or a couple of other felt pens for limited color effect. Quickly draw out some ideas of how you would deal with the problem. Just try to get a spontaneous feel for several kinds of solutions.

■ After you've drawn a bit you'll find things you like. Don't just toss these away and start anew. Use your tracing paper to overlay other sheets, evolving the best ideas to the top sheet, keeping the good parts of what you have and changing the other parts.

QUICK MODELS Another key design development tool is the rough or quick model. Using it you're designing a three-dimensional space within a three-dimensional visualizing aid. Keep it rough and temporary; when you begin to worry how it looks to others, you'll lose its value as a method in designing. In this way you can refine and develop your design. Once you have a good workable model, then you can create a presentation model. Find some materials that are easy to work with, such as chipboard and glue, or even cardboard. Many unsolvable design problems suddenly find a solution when the switch is made from flat paper to paper and cardboard models.

STAGE 2:
DESIGN COMMUNICATION

■ Effective communication of the design enables the client to visualize how his needs will be met by your solutions. He'll need to see your ideas from his vantage point, to see himself in the future with your completed design. That means you'll need to be as graphic as possible in your presentation of the idea. Because you and the client often are talking two different languages—visual and verbal—you'll need to bridge the gap by giving a visual presentation with verbal explanation. Clients don't like surprises. Your presentation should help him see as closely as possible what the design will look like when built or installed.

■ Before you start to draw the plans, set yourself certain standards. Determine consistency in your format. Use lettering in your labels; make clear and readable dimensions and descriptions. Keep line weights consistent. Look at the plans from the point of view of somebody who is reading them for the first time.

■ When you make a presentation, stress how the client will experience the spaces involved. Make your presentation professional. Realize that few clients are able to read floor plans and schematics correctly. Give them a realistic view of your design. Here are some aids to accomplish that.

THE KINDS OF CONSTRUCTION DRAWINGS

RENDERINGS These are colored, perspective drawings. They show the interior of the building as a person entering would see it. Included are representations of support material, people, and accessories. Renderings can be done in various media; the most often used are pencil, chalk, watercolor, tempera, felt pen, ink, or a combination. It's important to make the image believable, representative of how it really will look. Once the rendering has been made, it should be mounted on heavy board for the presentation.

FINAL MODELS In the development stage you probably made a model to help yourself work out details. Now you make a final model to show the client. This stage should probably not be used until the renderings are approved. The purpose of the model is to answer a client's questions and doubts, and to help him see even better what the final design will look like.

COLOR BOARDS These are presentations of the actual colors and materials that will be used in the interior you're creating. Color boards are created from mat or illustration board, on which you mount samples and pictures. Such items as carpet, drapery, tile, and wood can actually be mounted on the boards. Paint and other such items can be indicated by photographs or manufacturer's color samples. Color boards are very effective in giving the client a better understanding of what you're proposing. He can see depth and dimension; he can touch and feel the materials. And don't be upset if he doesn't like some of you samples. Use the color boards to narrow down what he *does* like, and save yourself a lot of trouble later.

PHOTOS

COLOR SWATCHES

TITLES

SLIDE PRESENTATIONS

■ Slides can be an effective way to show a client what you have in mind. You can show photos of your artwork, as well as examples of other buildings that do what you plan to do. When the client sees the pictures on the big screen they'll come alive for him and he'll be able to get a better image of it all.

■ To create a slide presentation, start by deciding where you want to begin and where you want to end. Then sit down and draw out a storyboard, a series of drawings that indicate what each slide will contain. Next, create a script that will show what you want to say with each slide. At that point you can start getting specific about exactly what you'll photograph. When you go in to make a slide presentation, be sure you're well prepared. Be familiar with the room you'll be using and be well acquainted with the equipment. Once you get proficient, you can consider using more than one projector, alternating slides or even superimposing them. Sound effects are a possibility. And when you're really comfortable with the medium you might think about making a movie presentation, showing the dynamics of the design, as well as the human scale next to an example of what you have in mind.

STAGE 3: CONSTRUCTION COMMUNICATION

■ After you talk to the client and get his go-ahead on the project, you'll need to start dealing with those who'll be doing construction, remodeling, and installation. The design is communicated with working drawings or a set of plans.

■ To communicate with construction people you'll need to be able to talk their language. They have their own point of view, their own unique approach to the business you sometimes share with them. If you can give them what they need you'll both be able to receive what you need.

FLOOR PLANS

■ Floor plans are a flat layout of the room. They are the most important thing you'll give the builder or installer. The critical thing to remember about floor plans is that they must be readable and they must be complete. By now you're very familiar with your design; you've probably fallen in love with it. But the floor plan is the builder's first exposure to it. Remember that, and *make it readable and complete.* A good floor plan will eliminate additional decisions—and it will aid cross referencing to the other papers you'll give the contractor.

COMMUNICATION

INTERIOR ELEVATIONS

These are vertical projections of the inside walls, particularly those that have cabinets or other special features attached to them. The builder will use these drawings to help him estimate the costs of the cabinet work and to help him know how to install them.

DETAILS

■ They are enlarged drawings of particular interior details that need special attention, such as cabinets, unique wall surfaces, built-in furniture, etc.

CROSS SECTIONS

■ Slice vertically through the building and look in: what you see is what you'll draw for your cross section. This will help the builder envision the building in its third dimension. There should be as many sections as the builder will need to have a complete view of the building. General cross sections will show the entire interior from a given point; smaller cross sections, drawn to larger scale, can show details of a smaller portion. With cross sections, the builder will know how to install stairs, how to deal with mouldings, and so on.

SCHEDULES

■ Every building has many elements that are important to it but that are not integral to the structure itself. Those elements are a vital part of the construction process, however. The schedule lists those parts of the building, tells what they're made of, and indicates where to put them. Every different kind of element will have a different schedule. For example, you might have a schedule, or list, of the doors in the building. It will indicate their size, what they're made of, where to get them, where to put them, how to finish them, and so forth. Other, separate schedules might deal with windows, floor coverings, appliances, and other such parts of the interior. The schedules of these elements are an important part of your communication with the builder. They're as essential to the successful completion of the product as the floor plan and specification sheet.

SPECIFICATIONS

■ The drawings you've been doing show the builder how to put together the different elements of the interior. The specifications show him exactly what those elements are. In other words, the specifications indicate the types of products, the quality of product

needed, and the particulars of craftsmanship. The specifications and the drawings work hand in hand to give the builder a more complete understanding of the interior design.

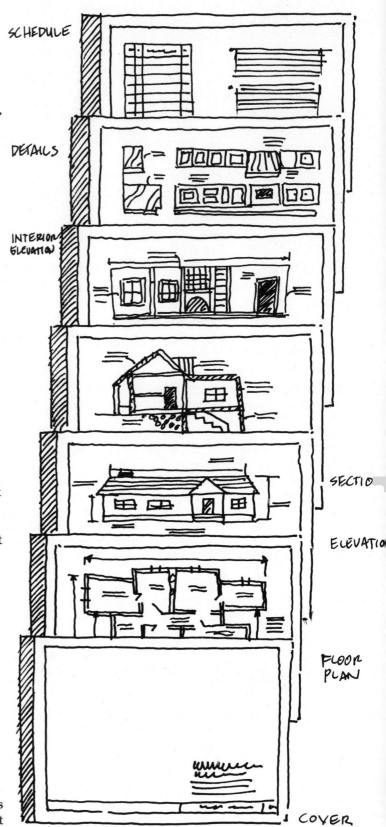

SCHEDULE

DETAILS

INTERIOR ELEVATION

SECTIO

ELEVATIO

FLOOR PLAN

COVER

INTERIOR DESIGN AS A BUSINESS

■ Even though in many ways interior design is an art, in the end the field must function as a business. As such, it acts like any other business. It has customers and it sells a service. If it is unable to attract customers—or to keep them satisfied—it will fail as a business, and those associated with it will be unable to practice their art. It is imperative, therefore, for every interior designer to use his skill to meet the needs of his clients and to promote the professionalism of his firm.

■ Some designers plan to get into the business and just *create* and *arrange*. The person who's able to limit his business dealings to that is rare—probably nonexistent. Instead you'll be handling paperwork, figuring estimates, placing orders, and maintaining records. You'll have to have an eye for detail and a willingness to follow through on the business aspects of your profession.

KINDS OF BUSINESSES

■ There are several ways you can enter the interior design business. The kind of business you associate yourself with will determine what kind of work you'll be doing.

1. **RETAIL ESTABLISHMENT** You could work for a department store, antique shop, furniture store, or furniture or textile manufacturer on a regular basis, doing the design work they need.

2. **ARCHITECTURAL, ENGINEERING, OR OTHER** firms. Oftentimes firms use resident interior designers.

3. **BUSINESS OFFICE** Some larger corporations use interior designers to help them with the many offices they build around the world.

4. **HOME STUDIO** You can go into business on your own, doing whatever kinds of work you like best—or can get.

There are certain basic services you'll probably perform wherever you work. Here is a listing of the kinds of things you should become proficient at:

- Scheduling projects, including all the details
- Consulting with architects and craftsmen
- Developing layouts and floor plans
- Preparing presentation drawings (used to show perspectives, and relationships, etc.; shown to client)
- Preparing working drawings (include all specifications; shown to architect, builder, fabricator, etc.)
- Coordinating all colors to be used
- Coordinating all three-dimensional elements to be used
- Knowing differences in paints and wall coverings
- Knowing differences in furnishings and accessories

PROFESSIONALISM

■ For many years people have made no distinction between the terms *interior designer* and *interior decorator,* a fact that has made many designers cringe. The distinction is one of professionalism: anyone can set up shop and be called an interior decorator. But to be acknowledged an interior *designer,* according to the guidelines of the national organizations, one must have at least the trappings of professionalism. That means the person must have a four-year college degree with an emphasis in design, as well as three or four years' experience in a "recognized establishment." Clearly, becoming a designer requires specialized qualifications. But the resulting professionalism is valuable.

■ More is expected of the person who is viewed as a professional. But in return he is given more trust and credibility. His word is accepted as more reliable; his judgment is viewed as having greater weight.

A PROFESSIONAL IMAGE

■ At times interior design has had to struggle to gain credibility and professional stature. This has been caused by the neglect and incompetence of a few. Design specialists must work together to give a more unified and controlled image of professionalism. Clients, peers, community leaders and others must come to view interior design as an area offering an important service from qualified experts. The projects designers are involved with, their levels of involvement, and their pay all relate to our image.

PAYMENT

One important consideration is how you'll be compensated for your efforts. There are six different ways you can be paid, and you'll have to work out for yourself which will be best for you.

1. **RETAIL BASIS** With this method you take the materials the client needs, which you get at wholesale, and mark them up to retail. Your markup can be as much as 100 percent, and that amount will cover the costs of your work. When you're dealing with stock work, this method can pay you the most. When you're dealing custom, it may not be as remunerative.

PROFESSIONAL

2. COST PLUS PERCENTAGE Here you add up all the costs of the materials, mark them up around 25 percent, and give that to the client as the bill. This method is commonly used by young designers who are trying to build a clientele—and it's the least remunerative of the six methods, If you want to use this method, add to it an hourly rate to pay for your time and talent.

3. PERCENTAGE OFF RETAIL With this approach you work from the manufacturer's list price for the materials you need to get, then discount the amount by 10 percent or so. This gives you a significantly greater profit than the cost plus percentage method, but still gives the client a better deal than he would get if he didn't use you.

4. FLAT FEE This method is not commonly in use, mainly because it contains so many hazards. With the flat fee, the designer quotes a specific amount the job will cost and sticks to it. The materials are billed directly to the client. The main problem with charging a flat fee is that all clients are different—and a good part of the designer's time is spent working directly with his client. If you choose this method, make sure you have an agreement with the client for precisely what will be done. Be sure the budget is set and immovable, since that will determine the job you do. And be certain that you consider all aspects of the job, so you'll know just how long it will take, and can figure your fee accordingly.

5. FLAT FEE PLUS PERCENTAGE To protect yourself against an expanding budget, you might try a variation of the flat fee approach. Charge your flat fee as agreed—but if the budget goes up, you charge a percentage of the cost on the additional amount. If the budget goes down, you'll have to do less work than you expected and will thus get the money you planned on with less effort.

6. HOURLY AND PER DIEM CHARGES This method is generally used in connection with other methods, and it's rarely used at all in the residential field. Usually you'd apply the hourly rate only on special services, such as consultations, time spent with the architect, time spent on preparing working drawings to solve a specific problem, and shopping time. Per diem charges might be applied to such things as travel to markets to find specific items requested by the client. Often you'd apply more than one method of charging for your work, since work conditions vary from one part of a job to another.

PROJECT DEVELOPMENT CHART

- On the bottom of the page is a typical development chart on dealing with a client on a project. A professional is not haphazard but uses a consistent and deliberate process towards the effective completion of a job.

- Successful design practices use similar processes but diverse approaches. Professionalism has common rules, a unified foundation, and a diversity of excellence.

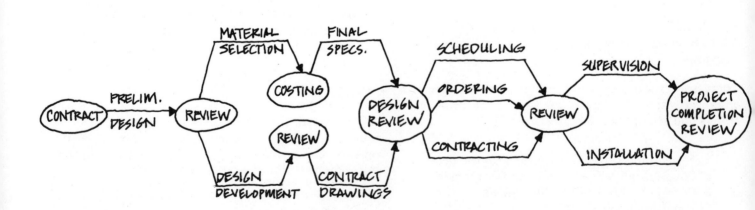

GETTING IDEAS

■ The world runs on ideas. Interior design runs on ideas. Those in the profession who are unable to develop new ideas are forever consigned to be imitators. And imitators are not quite good enough at their craft.

■ It's helpful to know that creative ideas are rarely new—they're just old concepts combined in a new and useful way. The electric toothbrush is just an electric motor and a toothbrush. Benjamin Franklin invented the bifocals—but he did so simply by combining two sets of lenses in the same frame.

"The ability to relate and to connect sometimes in odd and yet in striking fashion, lies at the very heart of any creative use of the mind, no matter in what field or discipline."

George J. Seidel

STEPS FOR GENERATING GOOD IDEAS

■ With each new project, interior designers are faced again with the problem of getting new ideas. Every client, every space, and every solution places new demands for innovation. Some designers think that they are at the mercy of their past successes; they design cliches instead of being creative. Good ideas are available to anyone who is open to them. Here are the steps to getting good ideas that will work for any interior designer.

STATE THE PROBLEM

■ You have to know what the problem is before you can come up with an idea for resolving it. Jonas Salk could not have developed the polio vaccine without first finding out what was causing the disease. *He had to know the problem before he could solve it.*

■ Here are a couple of hints to help you in this step:

1. **PUT YOUR STATEMENT OF THE PROBLEM IN WRITING** That helps to define better what needs to be solved.

2. **STATE THE REAL PROBLEM** Don't be misled by preconceived notions. For example, many people tried to solve the housekeeper's problems by improving the broom. But they were trying to solve the wrong problem. H.G. Booth came along and realized the problem wasn't poorly designed brooms; it was removing dirt. So he threw out the broom and invented the vacuum cleaner.

■ How a problem is stated exerts tremendous control over how it is solved. The definition of a problem can dictate a solution before creative thinking even begins. Don't confine yourself by trying to improve old methods that don't work well. Instead get to the real problem, and that will lead you to the real solution.

USE ALL POSSIBLE SOURCES

GATHER DATA

■ You can theorize all you want, but you won't be able to get anywhere until you learn all the facts. Where do you gather data? Here are some suggestions:

1. **FIND OUT EXACTLY WHAT THE CLIENT NEEDS** Find out his idiosyncracies and attitudes.

2. **FIND OUT THE MONETARY CONSTRAINTS**

3. **DEFINE THE USE OF THE DESIGN**

4. **CONSULT AVAILABLE PUBLICATIONS,** as well as professionals, to find out how similar problems have been solved in the past.

Follow those four steps and you'll have the base data you need to work with.

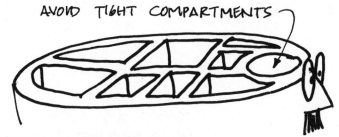

AVOID TIGHT COMPARTMENTS

DON'T COMPARTMENTALIZE

■ Once you have the basic facts, your first impulse will probably be to resolve the problem within the confines of the discipline of interior design. Don't! Often the best ideas come from outside sources. Gyorgy Kepes, a teacher and an artist, put it best: "The separation of our sensual, emotional and rational faculties into separate little slots is the prime reason for the formless nature of our environment and the lives we live." To get good ideas you need to eliminate the imaginary walls that separate the different areas of knowledge. As long as we separate our search for solutions into isolated compartments we suffer "hardening of the categories," and in the end fail to solve the problem creatively.

IDEATION

DEFER JUDGMENT

■ People who jump to conclusions often frighten the best ideas away. Getting ideas and judging their worth are two entirely different thought processes, and the two should not be mixed. Far too many good ideas have been sent to an early grave by the words, "It'll never work." When Chester Carlson, inventor of the electrostatic copy machine, tried to sell his idea, he met with what Carlson called "an enthusiastic lack of interest." But he was a rare one; he wouldn't accept the negative judgment of his idea. His perseverance resulted in the success story we call Xerox.

■ Give your ideas a chance to mature and grow—and to produce—before you judge them. You can't judge an apple until after it has ripened on the tree. The same is true of many an idea.

SELECT THE RIGHT MENTAL APPROACH

■ The problem-solving approach you take will vary according to your circumstances. If you're in a group, brainstorming is a good approach to try. If you're working something out by yourself, you'll be working only with your own mind—and your approach will vary accordingly.

■ Here are the rules for brainstorming:

1. Make sure everyone knows what you're going after.
2. Let everyone speak out his ideas; have someone assigned to write them down on a chalkboard or piece of paper.
3. Don't make a judgment on any of the ideas during the brainstorming session. That will kill the flow of ideas right off. Instead just write them down and judge them later.

■ Here are some rules for developing ideas on your own:
1. Make sure your brain knows precisely what you're going after.
2. Whenever you get an idea write it down. It's helpful to carry a notebook around for that purpose while you're working on a particular problem.
3. Write down any idea that comes to you. Don't judge it one way or the other until after the idea-collection time is over.

4. Put yourself in an environment where ideas are stimulated. A television show or a novel might be the worst thing for you when you're trying to solve something. Better might be to thumb through a book on interior design, just to take a look.
5. Don't force the process. Get the problem in your brain and then just let it cook for a while. The subconscious is often the source of our best ideas, and for some reason it doesn't work very effectively when the conscious is working on the same problem. Let yourself daydream.

■ As you can tell from the above, it's necessary to do the right kind of groundwork before you can get your best ideas. But it's also necessary to let the mind do its work. Henri Poincare said, "Creative ideas do not come to me while I am working at my desk, but usually flash into my head while I am engaged in other activities." What's true for him is true for all of us!

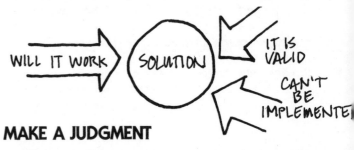

MAKE A JUDGMENT

■ You've gone through all the steps to get the idea and it has come. Now you need to decide whether or not the idea is valid. Up till now you've deferred your judgment. But the judgment has to be made, and it must be made before the idea is implemented.

■ How do you judge an idea? Go back to the list of items you made when you were gathering data. They'll give you the criteria for judging the idea you've come up with. You'll need to ask yourself how the solution fits with the client, how it fits with the use it will have, whether or not it accords with the monetary constraints, how well it fits with good taste.

■ If the idea works well with all those criteria, then it's time to implement it. If it doesn't, go back to Step 1 and start over!

IMPLEMENT THE IDEA

An idea will never do you any good unless you do something about it. Alex Osborn said, "The creative process does not end with an idea; it starts with one. Creative ideas are just the first step in a long process of bringing thoughts into reality." Now that you have your idea, get busy!

SOURCES OF IDEAS

No one exists in a vacuum. Good design, in the end, is interdependent: the person who does a good job in one area gets his ideas from others and modifies them; others in turn, learn from still other designers. This field is dynamic, not static, and those who succeed are continually learning from one another, continually developing skills as they observe the good work of others. Because of this, idea sources are critical for the person who would become proficient in the field of interior design. Those sources can bring inspiration, and can help the designer become more acquainted with the possiblities—and latest thoughts—in his field.

THE BEGINNER TRAPS

■ Most beginners in interior design fall into two groups. The first group uses their own limited experience as a basis for their design. The result is a continually repeated series of poor design cliches. Their creation, whatever the medium, is generally quite superficial and definitely unsatisfactory.

■ The second group also has failings. They study what's been done by other designers and try to duplicate it. The result is design—misplaced. Even though the basic design they're working with is successful (after all, they borrowed it from a successful designer!), the *use* of that design is unsuccessful.

■ But once they get a little design experience they're able to move into a more comfortable situation. Those who are good learners are able to develop a style that uses the best of the above two groups. They're able to combine their intuitive sense of design with an awareness of what has worked in the past. That, finally, results in a successful product. The best solutions are invariably a happy combination of new ideas that work with previous ideas that work.

REFERENCES FOR DESIGN

■ Here is a list of books and magazines you can refer to as you better develop your craft. These books and magazines are *sources* of ideas. They will help you as you seek the workable combination of the old with the new.

■ Certainly this list isn't the last word on interior design sources. New books are coming out all the time, and many of them will be quite helpful. So in your reading, range far and wide, deriving what you can from the publications in print.

REFERENCE WORKS

American Interiors
American Digest
Viking Press

Design from Scandinavia
Kirsten Bjerregaard
International School Book Service

The House Book
Terence Conran
Crown

Living Spaces
Franco Magrani
Watson-Guptill

Encyclopedia of Furniture
Joseph Avonson
Crown

Architectural Digest of Interiors
Parge Rense
Knapp Press

Residential Interiors
Catherine Crane
Watson-Guptill

Interior Spaces Designed by Architects
Architectural Record
McGraw-Hill

Drawings of Architectural Interiors
John Pile
Watson-Guptill

Specifications for Commercial Interiors
S. C. Reznikoff
Whitney

Architectural Graphic Standards
C.G. Ramsey and H.R. Sleeper
Wiley

INTERIOR DESIGN BOOKS

Beginnings of Interior Environment
Phyllis S. Allen
BYU Press

Interior Design: An Introduction to Architectural Interiors
Arnold Friedmann et al.
Elsevier

The Use of Color in Interiors
Albert O. Halse
McGraw-Hill

Architecture as a Home for Man
Lewis Mumford
McGraw-Hill

Interior Design Careers
R. Schneider
Prentice-Hall

Human Dimensions and Interior Space
Julius Panero
Watson-Guptill

Drawing as a Means to Architecture
William K. Lockard
Pepper Publishing

Techniques of Interior Design Rendering and Presentation
Sid Leach
Architectural Record Books

A Guide to Business Principles & Practices for Interior Designers
Herbert Stegel
Watson-Guptill

PERIODICALS

Architectural Digest
Interiors
Interior Design
The House Beautiful
Progressive Architecture
Architectural Record
Residential Interiors
Better Homes and Gardens

Contract Interiors
Antiques
Domus
CASA
ABITARE
Designers West
Canadian Interiors
Progressive Architecture

OTHER IDEAS

■ Sometimes the best design sources available are not in the field of design at all. For instance, by looking through visually oriented books you can get all kinds of ideas that might not be found in design books at all. Examples of books you should consider include visually oriented encyclopedias and dictionaries, photo books, and catalogs for furniture buyers and interior designers.

OCCUPATION

GETTING A JOB

■ In the end, your purpose in studying interior design is to get a job in the field. Don't expect to get a job as a full-fledged top professional. If you're seeking that, you're being unrealistic. Instead what you should be looking for is a job at the entry level of the profession. Once you've gotten in, you can work up, but first you've got to get in.

THE PERSON WHO HIRES AND FIRES

■ The key to getting a job is the employer. He has his own particular needs in filling that job—you've got to determine what those needs are and then show him that you are the one to fill them.

■ Employers interview scores of people, but they encounter few who ask what their needs are. Prospective employees who do ask may get the job, even though they may not be quite as skilled as some of the other applicants. Why? Because they recognize that everyone, no matter what his skills, must grow in a new job. Employers select the ones who are most interested in making that growth, an interest demonstrated by their desire to meet the employer's needs.

WITHIN THE EYE OF THE EMPLOYER

■ Remember that during an interview a prospective employer is going to get an immediate image of you. That image may be quite different from how you see yourself, or "how you really are." So you've got to take care to see that his image is a favorable one.

YOU

WHAT DOES THE EMPLOYER SEE IN YOU?

LOOK THE PART

How do you do that? First, *dress* the part. Look like the kind of person he's looking for. Second, *talk* the part. Converse intelligently. Third, be knowledgeable in the field. You might be the best person for that employer's job, but he'll never know it if you don't know the concepts and terminology of interior design. In addition, take along two things when you apply for a job: your *resume* and your *portfolio*.

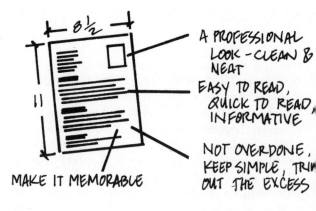

A PROFESSIONAL LOOK - CLEAN & NEAT

EASY TO READ, QUICK TO READ, INFORMATIVE

NOT OVERDONE, KEEP SIMPLE, TRIM OUT THE EXCESS

MAKE IT MEMORABLE

THE RESUME

■ The resume is a typed sheet giving the prospective employer a concise overview of your background. It should be up-to-date and professionally prepared, completely correct in terms of spelling, grammar, punctuation, and syntax. If you have weaknesses i any of those areas, get a friend or schoolteacher wh has those skills to help you.

■ No two resumes are the same. Each resume should be prepared for the audience in mind. If you plan to show your resume to school administrators so they'l hire you as an instructor, you'll prepare a resume emphasizing your teaching experience. If you plan to show it to the head of an interior design firm, you'll emphasize your experience in interior design.

■ Here are the things your resume should include:

PERSONAL Your name, address, and telephone numbe Your birthdate, marital status, and how many kids you have. A general statement on your health.

EDUCATION Note when you graduated from high school, and where. Note when and where you graduated from college; mention your major and minor. If you had a good grade-point average, make note of it. List two or three of the courses you took that would have critical bearing on the job in question. If you had special training in the military service or in seminars or workshops, say so. This section can give you a real boost if it's handled right. But remember to dwell only on information that has real bearing on the job in question. Anything else should get only the briefest mention.

WORK EXPERIENCE Starting with your most recent job, state your work experience, moving back to your earlier experience. Don't bother with part-time jobs you had in high school or college—unless they will help further your cause. An internship or summer job *can* be a help if they were in your field. You should merely make note of jobs you had that aren't in this or a related field; but with jobs that do relate, be specific about your job functions. And don't forget to tell about any supervisory duties—those indicate that your former employer trusted you and respected your abilities. One caution: the prospective employer may well contact any of the employers you mention on the list to get "unbiased" input. Keep that in mind, particularly if you and one of those former employers didn't get along.

OTHER EXPERIENCE Here include any experience you had in community or church service that would relate to the job you're trying to get.

AWARDS AND MEMBERSHIPS List any awards you've received in the field, and any societies or organizations you've belonged to. If you've been an officer in one of those organizations, note that.

REFERENCES You could say "References provided upon request." But it might be better simply to list your references. Go to several people who know you and who would have credibility with a prospective employer. Ask them for permission to list them as references. Some people to consider would include a former employer, a clergyman, a community businessman, a public servant. This section is crucial. The prospective employer doesn't know you from Adam—why should he believe anything you say? But if you can give him some other people to check with, people who know you well enough to make a judgment but who would at the same time be unbiased, you can quickly boost your credibility.

OTHER ITEMS Some people like to write their career goals into their resume, and some like to list two or three personal interests. Those are perfectly acceptable to include in your resume, but do so only if they'll help you reach your employment goal.

■ Many students leave school with some good training in a field but little or no practical experience. The kind of experience that's needed is hard to find. Too often the young student finds himself in a well-known double bind. He can't get hired until he gets experience—and he can't get experience until he gets hired! How do you find your way out of that vicious circle? Do anything you can to get that vital experience. Decorate your neighbors' and relatives' homes, charging them only for the materials they were going to buy anyway. List them

as clients. Go down to your local department store and volunteer your services for their display window. List them as a former client. Go to a local interior design firm and work for free for a while. The training and experience you get will be invaluable, even though they'll probably give you the "go-fer" duties. And then you can list them as part of your experience. If you'll put out some effort and a little ingenuity, you'll be able to get some of that valuable experience.

PORTFOLIO

■ The portfolio is used to provide the prospective employer or client with a visual demonstration of your skills. You can tell him how good you are until the day grows long, but he's not going to know what you can really do until you show him. When you're trying to get a job, a professional looking portfolio is worth a thousand self-promoting words!

■ What should your portfolio be like? Start by picking out samples of your very best work. You don't want the employer to see the steps of your development; you want him to see what you've developed *to*. Also try to include a variety of different kinds of work. But, just as important, tailor-make the portfolio so it fits with the kind of work you'll be doing for that employer or client. Consider whether you'll be doing interior design for offices, stores, residences, cars, or whatever, then create your portfolio accordingly. In addition, you want it to be unified, rather than to present a hodge-podge image of your abilities.

KINDS OF PORTFOLIOS

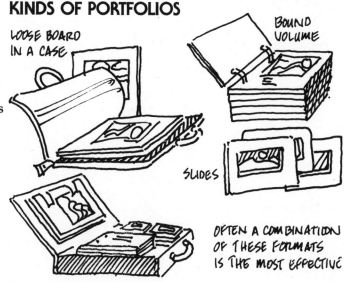

LOOSE BOARD IN A CASE

BOUND VOLUME

SLIDES

OFTEN A COMBINATION OF THESE FORMATS IS THE MOST EFFECTIVE

■ Ten to twenty pieces should be adequate for most portfolios. Less than that and the employer doesn't get enough feel for your work; more than that and he gets overloaded.

YOUR NOTES

■ The area of interior design will only be yours as you make it so. This notebook contains hundreds of principles and ideas on interior design; but these will all remain only so much stuff until you begin to internalize them. Start that process now by making notes on this page. What does interior design mean to you? What do you perceive as its most important principles? How can you be most successful as an interior designer? Write your thoughts in the space below and expand into your own notebook: